UTILIZING CANINE TEAMS TO DETECT EXPLOSIVES AND MITIGATE THREATS

HEARING

BEFORE THE

SUBCOMMITTEE ON TRANSPORTATION SECURITY

OF THE

COMMITTEE ON HOMELAND SECURITY

HOUSE OF REPRESENTATIVES

ONE HUNDRED THIRTEENTH CONGRESS

SECOND SESSION

JUNE 24, 2014

Serial No. 113-75

Printed for the use of the Committee on Homeland Security

Available via the World Wide Web: http://www.gpo.gov/fdsys/

U.S. GOVERNMENT PRINTING OFFICE

91–447 PDF   WASHINGTON : 2014

For sale by the Superintendent of Documents, U.S. Government Printing Office
Internet: bookstore.gpo.gov   Phone: toll free (866) 512–1800; DC area (202) 512–1800
Fax: (202) 512–2250   Mail: Stop SSOP, Washington, DC 20402–0001

COMMITTEE ON HOMELAND SECURITY

MICHAEL T. MCCAUL, Texas, *Chairman*

LAMAR SMITH, Texas
PETER T. KING, New York
MIKE ROGERS, Alabama
PAUL C. BROUN, Georgia
CANDICE S. MILLER, Michigan, *Vice Chair*
PATRICK MEEHAN, Pennsylvania
JEFF DUNCAN, South Carolina
TOM MARINO, Pennsylvania
JASON CHAFFETZ, Utah
STEVEN M. PALAZZO, Mississippi
LOU BARLETTA, Pennsylvania
RICHARD HUDSON, North Carolina
STEVE DAINES, Montana
SUSAN W. BROOKS, Indiana
SCOTT PERRY, Pennsylvania
MARK SANFORD, South Carolina
VACANCY

BENNIE G. THOMPSON, Mississippi
LORETTA SANCHEZ, California
SHEILA JACKSON LEE, Texas
YVETTE D. CLARKE, New York
BRIAN HIGGINS, New York
CEDRIC L. RICHMOND, Louisiana
WILLIAM R. KEATING, Massachusetts
RON BARBER, Arizona
DONDALD M. PAYNE, JR., New Jersey
BETO O'ROURKE, Texas
FILEMON VELA, Texas
ERIC SWALWELL, California
VACANCY
VACANCY

BRENDAN P. SHIELDS, *Staff Director*
JOAN O'HARA, *Acting Chief Counsel*
MICHAEL S. TWINCHEK, *Chief Clerk*
I. LANIER AVANT, *Minority Staff Director*

SUBCOMMITTEE ON TRANSPORTATION SECURITY

RICHARD HUDSON, North Carolina, *Chairman*

MIKE ROGERS, Alabama, *Vice Chair*
CANDICE S. MILLER, Michigan
SUSAN W. BROOKS, Indiana
MARK SANFORD, South Carolina
MICHAEL T. MCCAUL, Texas *(ex officio)*

CEDRIC L. RICHMOND, Louisiana
SHEILA JACKSON LEE, Texas
ERIC SWALWELL, California
BENNIE G. THOMPSON, Mississippi *(ex officio)*

AMANDA PARIKH, *Subcommittee Staff Director*
DENNIS TERRY, *Subcommittee Clerk*
BRIAN TURBYFILL, *Minority Subcommittee Staff Director*

CONTENTS

Page

UTILIZING CANINE TEAMS TO DETECT EXPLOSIVES AND MITIGATE THREATS

Tuesday, June 24, 2014

U.S. House of Representatives,
Subcommittee on Transportation Security,
Committee on Homeland Security,
Washington, DC.

The subcommittee met, pursuant to call, at 2:52 p.m., in Room 311, Cannon House Office Building, Hon. Richard Hudson [Chairman of the subcommittee] presiding.

Present: Representatives Hudson, Rogers, Brooks, and Richmond.

Mr. HUDSON. The Committee on Homeland Security's Subcommittee on Transportation Security will come to order. Subcommittee is meeting today to hear testimony on the use of canine teams to detect explosives and mitigate threats. I now recognize myself for an opening statement.

First, I would like to thank all of our witnesses for their participation. We know your time is valuable and we appreciate you being here today to discuss this important issue.

Most of us who have dogs know how incredibly intelligent and capable they are at detecting the slightest changes in their environments. When that intelligence is coupled with the highly selective breeding, months of intensive training, and breakthrough developments in science and technology, canines become one of the most trusted assets for law enforcement and military operations in critical environments. They serve as one of the most reliable security tools that exist today.

TSA has the second-largest number of explosive detection canine teams in the Federal Government, after the Department of Defense. TSA's National Explosives Detection Canine Team Program has a critical mission to deter and to detect the introduction of explosives into all the Nation's transportation systems.

With 985 teams today, including 675 teams handled by local law enforcement, and 310 teams handled by TSA inspectors, that is twice the number of teams that existed just 8 years ago. While we have come a long way in recent years, I believe TSA can and should continue to increase its use of canines in all aspects of its mission from passenger and baggage screening to air cargo screening.

One way TSA has diversified its canine program is by incorporating passenger screening canine teams into its risk-based security initiative known as Managed Inclusion. This initiative uses a combination of behavioral detection officers and passenger screening canine teams to conduct a real-time threat assessment of passengers at certain airports, to give them access to free check benefits on a flight-by-flight basis.

The canines used by TSA to conduct passenger screening represents a less invasive, highly effective approach. I would like to examine how canines can become a primary layer of security at airports, and not just used through Managed Inclusion, but as an every-day central layer of passenger screening operations.

In addition, TSA is working with other Federal entities to establish common guidelines and a baseline standard for Federal, State, local, and private-sector explosive detection canine assets. This committee and many stakeholders have long advocated for establishing common standards. I am hopeful that TSA will continue to make progress in this area.

I look forward to hearing from our TSA witnesses on whether common standards will help us move forward in providing the air cargo industry with the ability to utilize third-party canine teams to screen cargo. I believe we will hear from at least one of our witnesses today that this initiative is long overdue.

In January 2013 GAO released a report on TSA's canine program that offered three recommendations to TSA, including analyzing available areas that are working well and those that need corrective action, assessing overall effectiveness of passenger screening canines as compared to traditional canine teams, and coordinating with airport operators to deploy teams to the highest-risk airports.

GAO has informed the committee that it is prepared to close its first recommendation, and that TSA has made progress on addressing the other two recommendations. I look forward to receiving a status update from our GAO witness here today on this.

Finally, it is important to note that the fiscal year 2015 DHS appropriations bill that passed the House Appropriations Committee 2 weeks ago includes an additional $5 million for TSA canine teams, which will allow TSA to accelerate deployment and training of new teams. I am pleased to see this increase is included in the bill, and will continue to work with Chairman Carter and the rest of my colleagues to ensure full funding for this critical layer of security.

Again, I want to thank all of our witnesses for being here today. I now recognize the Ranking Member of the subcommittee, the gentleman from Louisiana, Mr. Richmond, for an opening statement.

Mr. RICHMOND. Thank you, Mr. Chairman. Thank you for convening this hearing.

I would also like to thank our panel of witnesses for being here today to give us valuable insight into TSA's use of canines and the role they play in aviation security for both passenger and cargo screening, as well as how they can be used more effectively in both domains.

The Transportation Security Administration ensures the security of the traveling public using a multi-layered approach. Highly-trained canine teams comprise a small part of this approach. But when used in an efficient and smart manner, they are an extremely effective tool within a larger toolbox that can thwart nefarious actors.

However, in January 2013 GAO released a report that was critical of TSA's handling of the roll-out of its passenger screening canines. Specifically the report stated that there was concern with the methodology that TSA implemented when deploying and testing the canine teams.

In their prepared testimony for the hearing today GAO noted that TSA is taking steps to analyze canine team data, and to identify program trends. I am eager to hear about the progress TSA has made in this regard, and also whether there is more that can be done by the agency to ensure that canine teams are being used in a thoughtful and efficient manner.

Ms. Harvey and Ms. Lontz, thank you for being here. Thank you for the role that you play in helping keep the traveling public secure.

I read your prepared testimony and was particularly interested in the section about the use of passenger screening canines in the Managed Inclusion process. You noted that these canine teams operate at more than 25 airports during peak travel times to help reduce waiting times. I know that these airports also have explosive trace detection equipment in place to perform the same function.

I look forward to learning if there are efficiencies that can be achieved by using one method over another or some combination of the two, as the cost for the technology as well as the passenger screening canines is great.

I am also interested in the role that explosive detection canine teams play in the maritime environment. As you know, New Orleans has a great deal of passengers who travel to and from the city to other destinations aboard cruise ships. I understand that most of the work performed in the maritime environment by canines is primarily in reference to ferries, but would be interested to know that the role that canines play in the screening of passengers and cargo aboard cruise ships such as during the VIPR operations.

Mr. Connell, thank you for appearing before the subcommittee today. I know that there is significant interest from the cargo screening industry in having privatized canines screen cargo as a means of having another platform available to detect threats.

I look forward to hearing about the screening methods that are already in place, as well as how the use of privatized canines would affect your operations, and what savings might stem from their use. I am also interested in the respondents to the survey you reference in your prepared testimony who indicated that they would not consider using dogs provided by private companies and why they would not use them.

Once again, thank you all for being here today. I look forward to a healthy dialogue on this topic.

With that, Mr. Chairman, I yield back the balance of my time.

[The statement of Ranking Member Richmond follows:]

STATEMENT OF RANKING MEMBER CEDRIC L. RICHMOND

JUNE 24, 2014

I would like to thank our panel of witnesses for being here today to give us valuable insight into TSA's use of canines and the role they play in aviation security for both passenger and cargo screening, as well as how they can be used more effectively in both domains.

The Transportation Security Administration ensures the security of the traveling public using a multi-layered approach. Highly-trained canine teams comprise a small part of this approach, but when used in an efficient and smart manner, they are an extremely effective tool within a larger toolbox that can thwart nefarious actors.

However, in January 2013, GAO released a report that was critical of TSA's handling of the roll-out of its passenger screening canines. Specifically, the report stated that there was concern with the methodology that TSA implemented when deploying and testing the canine teams. In their prepared testimony for the hearing today, GAO noted that TSA is taking steps to analyze canine team data and to identify program trends. I am eager to hear about the progress TSA has made in this regard and also whether there is more that can be done by the agency to ensure that canine teams are being used in a thoughtful and efficient manner.

Ms. Harvey and Ms. Lontz, thank you for being here, and thank you for the role that you play in helping keep the traveling public secure. I read your prepared testimony and was particularly interested in the section about the use of Passenger Screening Canines in the Managed Inclusion process. You noted that these canine teams operate at more than 25 airports during peak travel times to help reduce waiting times.

I know that these airports also have explosive trace detection equipment in place to perform the same function.

I look forward to learning if there are efficiencies that can be achieved by using one method over another, or some combination of the two, as the cost for the technology, as well as the passenger screening canines, is great. I am also interested in the role that explosive detection canine teams play in the maritime environment. As you know, New Orleans has a great deal of passengers who travel to and from the city to other destinations aboard cruise ships.

I understand that most of the work performed in the maritime environment by canines is primarily in reference to ferries, but would be interested to know the role that canines play in the screening of passengers and cargo aboard cruise ships, such as during VIPR operations.

Mr. Connell, thank you for appearing before the subcommittee today. I know that there is significant interest from the cargo screening industry in having privatized canines screen cargo as a means of having another platform available to detect threats. I look forward to hearing about the screening methods that are already in place, as well as how the use of privatized canines would effect your operations and what savings might stem from their use.

I am also interested in the respondents to the survey you referenced in your prepared testimony who indicated that they would not consider using dogs provided by private companies, and why they would not use them. Once again, thank you all for being here today, and I look forward to a healthy dialogue on this topic.

Mr. HUDSON. Thank the gentleman.

Other Members of the committee are reminded that opening statements may be submitted for the record.

[The statement of Ranking Member Thompson follows:]

STATEMENT OF RANKING MEMBER BENNIE G. THOMPSON

JUNE 24, 2013

In a time of shrinking budgets, TSA's canine program has the unusual distinction of having received increases in funding since fiscal year 2010. This year, TSA will spend $126 million to deploy canines to airports and mass transit hubs across the country. Increases in funding for TSA's canine program can be directly attributed to TSA's decision in 2011 to begin using canines to screen passengers and their property at airports.

Unfortunately, as the Government Accountability Office detailed in its report last year, TSA faced several challenges in its initial deployment of passenger screening canines. According to GAO, TSA failed to deploy passenger screening canine teams in a risk-based fashion and did not fully assess their effectiveness prior to placing them into the field.

While TSA has passenger screening canine teams placed at the most high-risk airports across the country today, a comprehensive assessment of their effectiveness has still not been conducted. Specifically, TSA has resisted GAO's recommendation that the agency conduct tests to determine whether passenger screening canines are more effective at identifying explosives on passengers than traditional, less costly, explosive detection canines.

Without conducting the assessment recommended by GAO, we can have no way of knowing whether the additional $18,000 per-team TSA is paying for passenger screening canines is money well-spent. With 144 passenger screening canine teams currently deployed, that extra $18,000 in start-up costs for each passenger screening canine team has already cost taxpayers more than $2.5 million. That is $2.5 million that TSA has no way of assuring us has been spent on a superior product.

I look forward to hearing from TSA today regarding their plans to address all of GAO's recommendations regarding passenger screening canines. I am also eager to hear from TSA about how canines serve as a better tool for reducing risk in the passenger screening environment than less-costly alternatives, such as explosive trace detection technology.

At some airports, TSA uses canines as part of its Managed Inclusion program. At others, it uses explosive trace detection technology for the same program and purpose. It must be asked, if the explosive trace detection technology is as effective at screening passengers for explosives as canines, why is the less-costly alternative not being used exclusively?

Before yielding back, I would like to acknowledge Mr. Connell's suggestion in his prepared testimony that TSA allow third-party canine teams to screen cargo carried on passenger aircraft. The 9/11 Act authorized TSA to approve the use of canines for screening cargo carried on passenger aircraft. It is my understanding that TSA is not opposed to allowing third-party canine teams to screen cargo on policy grounds but has concerns about the costs associated with performing oversight of such a regime.

I look forward to hearing from TSA regarding the anticipated cost associated with overseeing third-party canine screening. I am also eager to hear from Mr. Connell regarding how industry may be willing to offset the cost to taxpayers associated with the necessary Federal oversight of third-party private-sector canine screening of cargo.

Mr. HUDSON. We are pleased to have a distinguished panel of witnesses before us today.

Ms. Melanie Harvey is the division director of the Threat Assessment Division within the Office of Security Operations at TSA. As division director Ms. Harvey leads agency-wide efforts to plan, deploy, implement, and analyze real-time threat detection programs. Ms. Harvey manages policy, risk-based allocation, training, and quality assurance for TSA's explosives operations, behavior detection, and canine programs.

Ms. Annmarie Lontz is the division director for the Office of Law Enforcement's Office of Security Services and Assessments at TSA. Ms. Lontz joined the Federal Air Marshal Service in 1993, and has held her current position since July 2013, where she manages nine diverse sections within her office. Ms. Lontz was a special agent with the Federal Aviation Administration for 10 years and conducted investigations and security assessments domestically and internationally into airport and air carrier security.

Ms. Jennifer Grover is an acting director within GAO's Homeland Security and Justice team, leading a portfolio of work on transportation security issues. Prior to her work in Homeland Security and Justice, Ms. Grover was an assistant director in GAO's Health Care team, where she led her views on a diverse range of health-care related issues. Ms. Grover joined GAO in 1991.

Mr. Chris Connell is the president of Commodity Forwarders, Inc., and testifying on behalf of the Airforwarders Association. The Airforwarders Association is an alliance of nearly 400 indirect air carriers, cargo airlines, and affiliated businesses that serve as the voice of the airforwarding industry. Mr. Connell has been with Commodity Forwarders for 24 years, working in various positions in warehouses, customer service, and sales positions, culminating with him being named president in 2006.

The witnesses' full written statements will appear in the record. The Chairman now recognizes Ms. Harvey to testify.

STATEMENT OF MELANIE HARVEY, DIRECTOR, THREAT AS-SESSMENT DIVISION, TRANSPORTATION SECURITY ADMINISTRATION, U.S. DEPARTMENT OF HOMELAND SECURITY

Ms. HARVEY. Good afternoon, Chairman Hudson, Ranking Member Richmond, and Members of the subcommittee. Thank you for the opportunity to testify today regarding TSA's Explosive Detection Canine Teams and transportation security.

TSA's National Explosive Detection Canine Team Program trains and deploys both TSA-led and State and local-led canine teams in support of day-to-day activities that protect people and transportation. These highly-trained teams are an effective resource for detecting explosives and providing a visible deterrent to terrorism.

TSA canine teams are also a timely and noble response for rail stations, airports, passenger terminals, and surface carriers. They are a key component of TSA's multi-layered risk-based security model. The success of the canine program is a prime example of Federal, State, and local governmental entities working together to provide the most effective security in the most efficient way.

TSA's canine program has a storied history, beginning in 1972 with the creation of a unique program under the Federal Aviation Administration. The FAA canine program was transferred to TSA in 2003, shortly after its formation. Congress has recognized the value of TSA's program through continuous funding which has resulted in the largest explosive detection canine program in the Department of Homeland Security, and the second-largest in the Federal Government behind the Department of Defense.

Today, 985 funded canine teams are allocated to 171 locations in 114 cities across the country. TSA allocates these teams to specific cities and airports using risk-based criteria that take into account multiple factors including passenger throughput and threats to transportation security in the immediate geographical area.

The majority of our teams are comprised of a canine and a State or local canine handler. For these teams TSA provides and trains the dogs, trains the handler, provides training aides and explosive storage magazines, and conduct annual on-site canine team recertifications.

TSA partially reimburses each participating agency for operational costs associated with maintaining the teams. In return the State and local agencies agree to deploy the teams in their assigned transportation environment at least 80 percent of the handler's duty time. State and local participation in the program is voluntary and TSA appreciates the critical role that they play in securing transportation.

Some of TSA's own Transportation Security Inspectors, or TSIs, also handle canines. Approximately one-third of current canine teams are led by TSIs, including every one of the passenger screening canine teams, which are specifically trained to search people for explosives odor.

The passenger screening canine, or PSC, methodology is both complex and operationally demanding when compared to traditional explosive detection canine work. PSC handlers must have the ability to observe the canine and passengers while noticing the potential subtle changes in behavior of their canine while working in confined spaces.

As a result of their specialized training and capability, PSC teams play a unique role in risk-based security at TSA. In 2012 TSA expanded the PreCheck population through an initiative known as Managed Inclusion. By combining existing layers of security in the passenger queue, including PSC teams, TSA is making real-time threat assessments of the passenger base as they present for screening.

Currently TSA's PSC teams operate at 27 airports during peak travel times where they increase security and reduce wait times. Canine teams complement other checkpoint technologies that offer different capabilities, such as detection of other prohibited items and advanced alarm resolution.

The recommendations of the 9/11 Commission Act included a requirement for DHS to examine the use of third-party explosive detection canine teams for air cargo screening, and set performance standards. In 2011, in partnership with the DHS Science and Technology Directorate, TSA conducted a third-party pilot assessment to examine the use of these teams in the cargo environment.

TSA and DHS S&T analyzed current industry detection canine capabilities to determine the degree of modification needed to adopt and implement TSA standards. While there is little question that canine teams can effectively buy down risk when used to screen cargo, the pilot identified numerous requirements and challenges for program implementation.

Some of these challenges include industry's need for access to explosives, TSA oversight required for explosives handling, and the operational mechanics and resource requirements for certification evaluation of these teams on a Nation-wide scale.

In conclusion, TSA's National Explosives Detection Canine team is instrumental to risk-based security, and offers a unique capability to deter and detect explosives throughout transportation venues.

Thank you for the opportunity to discuss TSA's program with you today. I am pleased to answer your questions.

[The joint prepared statement of Ms. Harvey and Ms. Lontz follows:]

JOINT PREPARED STATEMENT OF MELANIE HARVEY AND ANNMARIE LONTZ

JUNE 24, 2014

Chairman Hudson, Ranking Member Richmond, and Members of the subcommittee, thank you for the opportunity to testify regarding explosives detection canine teams and transportation security. The mission of the Transportation Security Administration (TSA) is to protect the Nation's transportation systems to ensure freedom of movement for people and commerce. TSA's National Explosives Detection Canine Team Program (NEDCTP) trains and deploys both TSA-led and State and local law enforcement-led canine teams in support of day-to-day activities that protect the transportation domain. These highly-trained explosive detection canine teams have proven to be a reliable resource at detecting explosives and provide a visible deterrent to terrorism directed towards transportation systems. TSA canine teams are also considered a timely and mobile response for support facilities, rail stations, airports, passenger terminals, seaports, and surface carriers. They are a key component of TSA's risk-based security model and an important layer of TSA's multi-layered security program. The success of the NEDCTP is a prime example of Federal, State, and local governmental entities working together with a common goal—to help secure our Nation's transportation system.

TSA's NEDCTP has a storied history, beginning in 1972 with the creation of a unique Federal program, which established the Federal Aviation Administration's

(FAA) Explosives Detection Canine Team Program. The FAA program was designed to place certified teams at strategic locations throughout the Nation, so any aircraft receiving a bomb threat could quickly divert to an airport with a canine team. The FAA program was transferred to TSA in 2002, shortly after its formation, and has continued to expand. Congress has recognized the value of TSA's National Explosives Detection Canine Team Program through continuous funding which has resulted in the largest explosives detection canine program in the Department of Homeland Security (DHS) and the second-largest in the Federal Government behind the Department of Defense (DoD).

Today, 985 funded National Explosives Detection Canine teams are stationed at more than 100 of the Nation's airports, mass transit, and maritime systems. TSA trains canine teams to operate in the aviation, multimodal, maritime, mass transit, and cargo environments. The majority of canine teams working in the aviation environment are comprised of a dog and a local or State law enforcement officer. For these teams, TSA provides and trains the dog, trains the handler, provides training aides and explosive storage magazines, and conducts annual on-site canine team recertifications. TSA partially reimburses each participating agency for operational costs associated with maintaining the teams, including veterinarians' fees, handlers' salaries, dog food, and equipment. In return, the law enforcement agencies agree to use the canines in their assigned transportation environment at least 80 percent of the handler's duty time. State and local law enforcement participation in the program is voluntary, and they play a critical role in TSA's mission to ensure the safe movement of commerce and people throughout the Nation's transportation security environment.

PASSENGER SCREENING CANINES (PSCS) AND MANAGED INCLUSION (MI)

TSA's Transportation Security Inspectors (TSIs) also lead canine teams. Approximately one-third of current canine teams are led by TSIs, including every one of the 144 funded Passenger Screening Canine teams, which are specifically trained to detect explosives' odor on passengers in the checkpoint environment in addition to their conventional role.

As a result of their proven effectiveness, Passenger Screening Canine teams play a unique role in Risk-Based Security at TSA. In 2013, TSA expanded the TSA PreCheck™ population through the use of real-time threat assessments in an initiative known as Managed Inclusion. By combining existing layers of security in the passenger queue, including Passenger Screening Canines, TSA is making real-time threat assessments of the passenger base as they present for screening. This enables TSA to more fully utilize TSA PreCheck™ screening lanes in airports where they are not able to operate at their full TSA PreCheck™ capacity. Currently, TSA Passenger Screening Canine teams operate at more than 25 airports as part of Managed Inclusion and are deployed to operate during peak travel times, where they will have the opportunity to screen as many passengers as possible, helping to reduce wait times.

In addition to deployments at the checkpoints supporting the Managed Inclusion process, all TSA and law enforcement-led teams conduct a variety of search and high-visibility activities that address potential threats in the transportation domain. For example, canine teams play a role during Visible Intermodal Prevention and Response (VIPR) operations. VIPR teams can include a variety of Federal, State, and local law enforcement and security assets as well as TSA personnel including Federal Air Marshals, Transportation Security Specialists—Explosives, Transportation Security Inspectors, and TSA-certified explosives detection canine teams.

At airports, TSA-led canine teams conduct risk-driven operations to address potential vulnerabilities in aviation security that are airport-specific, including no-notice plane-side screening of cargo, gate screening, and employee screening at high-volume secured area access points. These vulnerabilities are often identified through coordination with local or National security partners, including the Federal Bureau of Investigation, local law enforcement, and the National Targeting Center for Cargo.

Canine teams have been proven to be one of the most effective means of detecting explosive substances. Canine teams complement other technologies that offer expanded capabilities in terms of detecting other prohibited items, including firearms.

DEPLOYMENT, ACQUISITION, AND TRAINING

TSA allocates canine teams to specific cities and airports utilizing risk-based criteria that take into account multiple factors, including passenger throughput and threats to transportation security in the immediate geographical area of a transportation domain.

With increasing demand for high-quality explosive detection dogs, particularly those best-suited for passenger screening, TSA must ensure a reliable and adequate supply of canines. The primary source for TSA canines is through an Interagency Service Support Agreement (ISSA) with the DoD. Pursuant to the terms of the ISSA and as a result of our strong relationship with DoD's "Working Dog Program," approximately 230 canines are supplied to TSA each year. TSA's Canine Training and Evaluation Section (CTES) partners with DoD during the canine selection and evaluation process with both State-side vendors and overseas buy trips, ensuring TSA's needs are met. TSA is well-positioned to procure, train, and continue to deploy highly-effective canine resources.

NEDCTP deploys single-purpose explosive detection canines that are trained on a variety of explosives. The types of explosives are based on intelligence data and emerging threats. Conventional explosives detection canine handlers undergo an intensive 10-week training course, and passenger screening canine handlers undergo a 12-week training course, all held at the TSA Canine Training Center at Lackland Air Force Base in San Antonio, TX. This course of instruction is a "co-located course," managed by TSA's CTES, whereby TSA shares the use of the U.S. Air Force training facilities on base. However, TSA controls the course curriculum and the certification of the teams to TSA-certification standards. The training course and facilities in San Antonio, Texas, are considered to be the "Center of Excellence" for explosives detection canine training in the United States.

Canine teams graduate from the TSA canine course after demonstrating proficiency in various venues inclusive of all transportation environments including airport, terminal, freight, cargo, baggage, vehicle, bus, ferry, and rail. Once a team graduates from the training program, they return to their duty station to acclimate and familiarize the canine to their assigned operational environment. Approximately 30 days after graduation, an Operational Transition Assessment (OTA) is conducted to ensure each team demonstrates operational proficiency in their environment. OTA assessments include four key elements: The canine's ability to recognize explosives odors, the handler's ability to interpret the canine's change of behavior, the handler's ability to conduct logical and systematic searches, and the team's ability to locate the explosives odor source. Upon successful completion of the OTA, NEDCTP canine teams are then evaluated on an annual basis under some of the most stringent certification standards.

INTERNATIONAL SECURITY PROGRAMS

In 2013, TSA established and implemented a formal process for evaluating and recognizing National Explosives Detection Canine Security Programs (K9 SPs) in foreign countries for use in aviation security, checked baggage, and accessible property. Recognition of K9 SPs has several benefits; it allows for greater facilitation of goods, commerce, and people between countries and eases the burden on industry by lifting, where appropriate, duplicative or redundant measures while still ensuring the highest levels of security. TSA has conducted formal document reviews of several international partners to include New Zealand, the European Union, and South Africa. In order to recognize National canine security programs as commensurate with the components of the TSA canine program, TSA employs a system-to-system approach when reviewing a canine security program. This system-to-system approach involves analysis of a host country's security program using a framework of five fundamental security criteria: Explosive detection certifications, training, utilization, explosives training aids, and oversight and compliance. The approach ensures that the combination of the components that make up a host country's security program provide a level of security that is commensurate with the components of the TSA Canine Program's own security system. To date, TSA continues to receive requests for recognition from international canine programs.

THIRD-PARTY CANINE

Recommendations of the 9/11 Commission Act of 2007 directed DHS to examine the use of third-party explosive detection canine teams for air cargo screening. In 2011, TSA, in coordination with the DHS Science and Technology Directorate (S&T), conducted a Third-Party Pilot Assessment to examine the use of these teams in the cargo environment. TSA and DHS S&T analyzed current industry detection canine capabilities through a pilot to determine the degree of modification to industry programs needed to adopt and implement TSA screening standards. The assessment revealed inconsistent results of industry programs due to unsatisfactory odor recognition and performance. However, TSA remains open to future proposals on third-party canine use.

INDUSTRY COLLABORATION

TSA has partnered with the National Security Staff Transborder Security Sub-Interagency Policy Committee on Working Dogs to establish a baseline standard for Federal, State, local, and private-sector explosives detection canine assets to enhance interoperability of standards for explosives detection canine team programs. Currently, the committee is working towards a final time line for final coordination, clearance, and limited publication of the draft guidelines in the *Federal Register*.

CONCLUSION

In conclusion, the National Explosives Detection Canine Program provides highly-trained canine teams focused on furthering TSA's mission to secure the Nation's transportation systems. They are instrumental in risk-based security and offer a unique capability to deter and detect explosives throughout transportation venues. Thank you for the opportunity to discuss this important issue with you today.

Mr. HUDSON. Thank you, Ms. Harvey.

The Chairman recognizes Ms. Lontz to testify.

STATEMENT OF ANNMARIE LONTZ, DIVISION DIRECTOR, OFFICE OF SECURITY SERVICES AND ASSESSMENTS, TRANSPORTATION SECURITY ADMINISTRATION, U.S. DEPARTMENT OF HOMELAND SECURITY

Ms. LONTZ. Chairman Hudson, Ranking Member Richmond, and Members of the subcommittee, I too would like to thank you for the opportunity to testify today regarding TSA's Explosives Detection Canine Teams and transportation security.

As the division director for the TSA Office of Law Enforcement Federal Air Marshal Service, Security Services and Assessments Division, I am charged with the oversight of the Canine Training and Evaluation Section, located primarily at Lackland Air Force Base in San Antonio, Texas.

The Canine Training and Evaluation Section, or CTES, supports Division Director Harvey's National Explosives Detection Canine Team Program through the procurement of canines, initial training and certification of canine teams, and recertification of deployed canine teams.

With increasing demand for a high-quality explosive detection dogs, particularly those best-suited for passenger screening, TSA must ensure a reliable and adequate supply of canines. The primary source for TSA canines is through an interagency service support agreement with the Department of Defense. Pursuant to the terms of the agreement, and as a result of our strong relationship with DOD's working dog program, approximately 230 canines are supplied to TSA each year.

TSA's Canine Training and Evaluation Section partners with DOD during the canine selection and evaluation process, both with State-side and international vendors, ensuring that TSA's needs are met. As a result, TSA is well-positioned to procure, train, and continue to deploy highly-effective canine resources.

TSA deploys explosive detection canines that are trained on a variety of explosives, primarily based on intelligence data and emerging threats. Conventional explosives detection canine handlers undergo an intensive 10-week training course, and passenger screening canine handlers undergo an additional 2 weeks for a total of 12 weeks of training. All is held at the TSA Canine Training Center at Lackland Air Force Base.

This course of instruction is a co-located course managed by TSA's CTES, whereby TSA shares the use of the U.S. Air Force training facilities on base. However, TSA controls the course curriculum and the certification of the teams to TSA's certification standards. The training course and facilities in San Antonio, Texas are considered to be the Center of Excellence for explosive detection canine training in the United States.

Canine teams graduate from the TSA canine course after demonstrating proficiency in various venues inclusive of all transportation environments including airport, terminal, freight, cargo, baggage, vehicle, bus, ferry, and rail. Once a team graduates from the training program they return to their duty station to acclimate and familiarize the canine to their assigned operational environment.

Approximately 30 days after graduation an Operational Transition Assessment is conducted to ensure that each team demonstrates operational proficiency in their environment. Operational Transition Assessments include four key elements: The canine's ability to recognize explosive odors; the handler's ability to interpret the canine's change of behavior; the handler's ability to conduct logical and systematic searches; and the team's ability to locate the explosive odor source.

Upon successful completion of the OTA, the National Explosive Detection Canine Program teams are then evaluated on an annual basis under some of the most comprehensive certification standards requiring that they demonstrate their ability to detect all the explosives to which they may potentially be exposed.

TSA's highly-trained Explosive Detection Canine Teams have proven to be a reliable resource at detecting explosives and providing a visible deterrent to terrorism. The Canine Training and Evaluation Section plays an important role in the deployment of these canine teams, focused on furthering TSA's mission to secure the Nation's transportation systems.

Thank you for the opportunity to discuss this important issue with you today.

Mr. HUDSON. Thank you, Ms. Lontz.

The Chairman recognizes Ms. Grover to testify.

STATEMENT OF JENNIFER A. GROVER, ACTING DIRECTOR, HOMELAND SECURITY AND JUSTICE, GOVERNMENT ACCOUNTABILITY OFFICE

Ms. GROVER. Good afternoon, Chairman Hudson, Ranking Member Richmond, and other Members and staff. I am pleased to be here today to discuss TSA's implementation and oversight of the National Explosives Detection Canine Team Program.

TSA has deployed over 800 canine teams, including conventional canines, which detect explosives in stationary objects, and passenger screening canines, known as PSCs, which receive additional training to detect and track explosives being carried on a person.

As you noted earlier, in January 2013 GAO reported on concerns in three areas. First, TSA's insufficient oversight of the canine program overall. Second, lack of evidence on the effectiveness of PSCs in the airport environment, and third the inconsistent implementation of TSA's policy for risk-based deployment of PSCs.

Since then TSA has taken steps in all three areas. But TSA has yet to determine if conventional canines can perform the same function as PSCs with the same results and at lower cost.

Regarding our first finding about weakness in program oversight, in 2013 we reported that TSA was collecting data, but not analyzing it over time to identify areas working well or in need of correction. For example, when we analyzed the TSA data we found that some canine teams repeatedly did not meet training requirements.

Also, TSA was not analyzing their covert test results beyond a simple pass-and-fail rate. As a result, TSA was missing the chance to identify specific search areas or types of explosives where the canine teams were more or less effective. We recommended that TSA regularly analyze their data to better understand canine proficiency and ensure effective program operations.

Now since then TSA has started analyzing canine program data in all the areas highlighted in our review. In fact, 3 months ago they staffed a new office within TSA called the Performance Measurements Section, which is focused specifically on improving the management and oversight of the canine program by analyzing the canine team data.

Regarding our second finding on effectiveness, in 2013 we reported that TSA had started using the PSCs in the sterile areas of the airports, before determining their effectiveness and before determining where in the airport they would be most effectively used.

We also noted that TSA's testing had raised questions about whether conventional canines might outperform the PSCs under certain airport testing scenarios, and thus recommended that TSA comprehensively assess the effectiveness of the PSC and the conventional canine teams.

In response, TSA took action to assess the effectiveness of PSC teams, and they determined that the PSCs are effective when working at the airport checkpoints. However, TSA has not compared the relative effectiveness of the PSC and the conventional canines at the airport checkpoint, which is important to ensure that the additional resources that are required for the PSC teams are warranted.

Finally regarding deployment, in 2013 we found that TSA was not consistently deploying PSC teams to the highest-risk airports. At the time TSA officials told us that they generally defer to airport officials regarding PSC deployment, and that some airports had concerns about the use of the PSC teams, specifically related to the composition of the teams and implication should a PSC team detect explosives on a person.

We recommended that TSA coordinate with airport stakeholders to deploy PSC teams to the highest-risk airports. TSA agreed, and they have since deployed or committed to deploy additional PSC teams to the highest-risk airports.

As we heard today, TSA has also reported that some airports previously opposed to the use of PSCs have accepted them as part of the Managed Inclusion program, which allows passengers not enrolled in TSA PreCheck to access the PreCheck's screening lanes in certain circumstances.

In conclusion, TSA's new emphasis on data analysis will better position the agency to understand how well the program is working, and to target program resources accordingly. Importantly, a comprehensive assessment of the relative effectiveness of PSCs and conventional canines is still necessary to provide assurances that the PSC canines are a cost-effective screening tool.

Chairman Hudson, Ranking Member Richmond, this concludes my statement. I look forward to your questions.

[The prepared statement of Ms. Grover follows:]

PREPARED STATEMENT OF JENNIFER GROVER

JUNE 24, 2014

GAO HIGHLIGHTS

Highlights of GAO–14–695T, a testimony before the Subcommittee on Transportation Security, Committee on Homeland Security, House of Representatives.

Why GAO Did This Study

TSA has implemented a multi-layered system composed of people, processes, and technology to protect the Nation's transportation system. One of TSA's security layers is NEDCTP, composed of over 800 deployed explosives detection canine teams, including PSC teams trained to detect explosives on passengers.

This testimony addresses the extent to which TSA has: (1) Regularly analyzed data to identify program trends and areas working well or in need of corrective action, and (2) comprehensively assessed the effectiveness of PSCs, and coordinated with stakeholders to deploy PSC teams to the highest-risk airports and utilize them as intended. This statement is based on a report GAO issued in January 2013 and selected updates obtained from October 2013 through June 2014. For the selected updates, GAO reviewed TSA documentation, including the results of PSC effectiveness assessments, and interviewed agency officials on the status of implementing GAO's recommendations.

What GAO Recommends

GAO is making no new recommendations in this statement.

EXPLOSIVES DETECTION CANINES.—TSA HAS TAKEN STEPS TO ANALYZE CANINE TEAM DATA AND ASSESS THE EFFECTIVENESS OF PASSENGER SCREENING CANINES

What GAO Found

In January 2013, GAO reported that the Transportation Security Administration (TSA) collected and used key canine program data in support of its National Explosives Detection Canine Team Program (NEDCTP), but could better analyze these data to identify program trends. For example, GAO found that in reviewing short notice assessments (covert tests), TSA did not analyze the results beyond the pass and fail rates. Therefore, TSA was missing an opportunity to determine if there were any search areas or types of explosives in which canine teams were more effective compared with others, and what, if any, training may be needed to mitigate deficiencies. GAO recommended that TSA regularly analyze available data to identify program trends and areas that are working well and those in need of corrective action to guide program resources and activities. TSA concurred and has taken actions that address the intent of our recommendation. For example, in the event a team fails a short-notice assessment, TSA now requires that canine team supervisors complete an analysis of the team's training records to identify an explanation for the failure.

In January 2013, GAO found that TSA began deploying passenger screening canine (PSC) teams—teams of canines trained to detect explosives being carried or worn on a person—in April 2011 prior to determining the teams' operational effectiveness and where within an airport PSC teams would be most effectively utilized. GAO recommended that TSA expand and complete testing to assess the effectiveness of PSCs and conventional canines (trained to detect explosives in stationary objects) in all airport areas deemed appropriate prior to making additional PSC deployments. This would help: (1) Determine whether PSCs are effective at screening passengers, and resource expenditures for PSC training are warranted, and (2) inform decisions regarding the type of canine team to deploy and where to optimally deploy such teams. TSA concurred and has taken steps to address the recommendation, but additional action is needed. Specifically, TSA launched a PSC training and assessment initiative and determined PSCs to be most effective when working at the airport checkpoint, but TSA does not plan to conduct a comparison of PSC teams with conventional canine teams as GAO recommended. In January 2013, GAO also found that TSA's 2012 Strategic Framework calls for the deployment of PSC teams based on risk; however, airport stakeholder concerns related to the composition and capabilities of PSC teams resulted in the teams not being deployed to the highest-risk airports. GAO recommended that if PSCs are determined to provide an enhanced security benefit compared with conventional canine teams, TSA should coordinate with airport stakeholders to deploy future PSC teams to the highest-risk airports. TSA concurred and has taken steps to address the recommendation. Specifically, the PSC teams for which TSA had funding and not already deployed to a specific airport at the time GAO's report was issued have been deployed to, or allocated to, the highest-risk airports.

Chairman Hudson, Ranking Member Richmond, and Members of the subcommittee: I appreciate the opportunity to discuss our work on the Transportation Security Administration's (TSA) National Explosives Detection Canine Team Program (NEDCTP). Within the Department of Homeland Security (DHS), TSA is the primary Federal agency responsible for security of the Nation's transportation system. Since the terrorist attacks of September 11, 2001, TSA has implemented a multi-layered system of security composed of people, processes, and technology to protect the transportation system. One of TSA's security layers is NEDCTP, composed of over 800 explosives detection canine teams—a canine paired with a handler—aimed at deterring and detecting the use of explosive devices in the U.S. transportation system.[1]

Through NEDCTP, TSA trains, deploys, and certifies explosives detection canine teams. The program began under the Federal Aviation Administration in 1972 as a partnership with State and local law enforcement agencies with jurisdiction over airports by pairing law enforcement officer (LEO) handlers with conventional canines trained to detect explosives in objects (e.g., baggage and vehicles). In accordance with the Aviation and Transportation Security Act, which established TSA, the transfer of the canine program from the Federal Aviation Administration to TSA was accomplished in March 2003.[2] TSA subsequently expanded the program beyond airports to other transportation modes, including mass transit, and in January 2008, further expanded the program to include civilian transportation security inspector (TSI) canine teams responsible for screening air cargo. In 2011, TSA again expanded the program by deploying TSI handlers to airports with passenger screening canines (PSC)—conventional canines also trained to detect explosives being carried by or worn on a person.

My testimony today addresses the extent to which TSA has: (1) Regularly analyzed data to identify program trends and areas working well or in need of corrective action; and (2) comprehensively assessed the effectiveness of PSCs, and coordinated with stakeholders to deploy PSC teams to the highest-risk airports and utilize them as intended. This statement is based on our January 2013 report and includes selected updates on the status of TSA's efforts to implement the recommendations in that report.[3] The report cited in this statement provides detailed information on our scope and methodology. To update our work, we obtained related documentation from TSA from October 2013 through June 2014, including reports used by NEDCTP to monitor canine team training minute requirements, results of PSC effectiveness assessments, and PSC deployment schedules. We also interviewed agency officials in June 2014 on the progress made by TSA to implement the recommendations in our January 2013 report. The work upon which this statement is based was conducted in accordance with generally accepted Government auditing standards. Those standards require that we plan and perform the audit to obtain sufficient, appropriate evidence to provide a reasonable basis for our findings and conclusions based on our audit objectives. We believe that the evidence obtained pro-

---

[1] NEDCTP is located within TSA's Office of Security Operations.

[2] Enacted in November 2001, the Aviation and Transportation Security Act established, within the Department of Transportation, TSA as the agency responsible for securing the Nation's transportation systems. See Pub. L. No. 107–71, § 101(a), 115 Stat. 597 (2001). The Homeland Security Act of 2002 subsequently transferred TSA to the newly-established Department of Homeland Security. See Pub. L. No. 107–296, § 403, 116 Stat. 2135, 2178 (2002).

[3] GAO, *TSA Explosives Detection Canine Program: Actions Needed to Analyze Data and Ensure Canine Teams Are Effectively Utilized*, GAO–13–239 (Washington, DC: Jan. 31, 2013). This is a public version of a sensitive report that we issued in December 2012. Information TSA deemed Sensitive Security Information was redacted.

vides a reasonable basis for our findings and conclusions based on our audit objectives.

BACKGROUND

NEDCTP's mission is to deter and detect the introduction of explosive devices into the transportation system. As of June 2014, NEDCTP has deployed 802 of 985 canine teams for which it is able to fund across the transportation system.[4] Table 1 shows the number of canine teams by type for which funding is available, as well as describes their roles, responsibilities, and costs to TSA. There are four types of LEO teams: Aviation, mass transit, maritime, and multimodal, and three types of TSI teams: Air cargo, multimodal, and PSC.

---

[4] NEDCTP has not deployed the remaining 183 canine teams.

TABLE 1.—TOTAL NUMBER AND FEDERAL COSTS OF TRANSPORTATION SECURITY ADMINISTRATION (TSA) CANINE TEAMS BY TYPE OF TEAM

Type of Canine Team	Number of Teams For Which Funding Is Available [1]	Description of Roles and Responsibilities	TSA Start-up Costs [2]	TSA Annual Costs [2]
Law enforcement officer (LEO): aviation.	511	Patrol airport terminals, including ticket counters, curbside areas, and secured areas; respond to calls to search unattended items, such as vehicles and baggage; screen air cargo; and serve as general deterrents to would-be terrorists or criminals.	$94,000	$63,000
LEO: mass transit	131	Patrol mass transit terminals; search platforms, rail cars, and buses; respond to calls to search unattended items, such as baggage; and serve as general deterrents to would-be terrorists or criminals.	$84,000	$53,000
LEO: maritime	6	Conduct similar activities as LEO mass transit teams at ferry terminals.	$84,000	$53,000
LEO: multimodal	27	Patrol and search transportation modes in their geographic area (e.g., aviation, mass transit, and maritime), and screen air cargo.	$94,000	$53,000
Transportation security inspector (TSI): air cargo.	120	Primarily screen air cargo	$218,000	$159,000
TSI: multimodal	46	Patrol and search transportation modes in their geographic area (e.g., aviation, mass transit, or maritime), and screen air cargo.	$218,000	$159,000
TSI: Passenger Screening Canines.	144	Search for explosives odor on passengers in airport terminals	$237,000	$164,000
Total	985			

Source: GAO analysis of TSA data. GAO–14–695T

[1] The number of teams for which funding is available is for fiscal year 2014.

[2] The cost data are as of June 2014, and have been rounded to the nearest thousand. Start-up costs reflect the costs incurred by TSA during the first year the canine team is deployed. Annual costs include the operations and maintenance costs incurred by TSA to keep canine teams deployed after their first year in the program.

TSA's start-up costs for LEO teams include the costs of training the canine and handler, and providing the handler's agency a stipend.[5] The annual costs to TSA for LEO teams reflect the amount of the stipend.[6] TSA's start-up and annual costs for TSI canine teams are greater than those for LEO teams, because TSI handlers are TSA employees, so the costs include the handlers' pay and benefits, service vehicles, and cell phones, among other things. PSC teams come at an increased cost to TSA compared with other TSI teams because of the additional 2 weeks of training and costs associated with providing decoys (i.e., persons pretending to be passengers who walk around the airport with explosive training aids). Of amounts appropriated in fiscal year 2014, TSA received a total of approximately $126.3 million for its canine program.[7] This amount includes an additional $1.25 million above TSA's fiscal year 2014 budget request to support not fewer than 10 more canine teams for the air cargo and aviation regulation environments.[8] In its fiscal year 2015 budget request, TSA is requesting approximately $127.4 million, a $1 million increase.[9]

Figure 1: Various Types of Canine Teams

Law enforcement officer team patrolling mass transit terminal — Transportation security inspector team screening air cargo — Passenger screening canine team searching airport terminal

Source: GAO | GAO-14-695T

Canines undergo 10 weeks of explosives detection training before being paired with a handler at TSA's Canine Training and Evaluation Section (CTES), located at Lackland Air Force Base. Conventional canine handlers attend a 10-week training course, and PSC handlers attend a 12-week training course.[10] Canines are paired with a LEO or TSI handler during their training course. After canine teams complete this training, and obtain initial certification, they acclimate to their home operating environment for a 30-day period. Upon completion of the acclimation period, CTES conducts a 3-day operational transitional assessment to ensure canine teams are not experiencing any performance challenges in their home operating environment. After initial certification, canine teams are evaluated on an annual basis to maintain certification. During the conventional explosives detection evaluation, canine teams must demonstrate their ability to detect all the explosive training aids the canines were trained to detect in five search areas.[11] The five search areas are

---

[5] The annual stipend is the Federal cost share TSA provides per LEO team pursuant to a cooperative agreement between TSA and the LEO team's agency (State or local). Certain items and services are reimbursable by TSA through the stipend, including canine food and veterinary care. The LEO team's agency is responsible for any costs incurred greater than the amount covered by the stipend.

[6] The LEO aviation teams' stipends are $10,000 more than those for other LEO teams because the teams are required to spend 25 percent of their time screening air cargo, per the cooperative agreement with TSA.

[7] For fiscal year 2014, TSA funds NEDCTP through three TSA activities: Aviation regulation and other enforcement (aviation), surface transportation security inspectors and canines (surface), and air cargo.

[8] See, e.g., Explanatory Statement accompanying Pub. L. No. 113–76, Div. F, 128 Stat. 5, 247 (2014), at 32.

[9] In its fiscal year 2015 budget request, TSA proposes to consolidate all canine assets, including PSC teams and mass transit teams, within its Aviation Regulation and Other Enforcement account to allow TSA maximum flexibility to utilize the teams in any transportation environment as needed in response to changes in intelligence or capability requirements.

[10] The majority of canine teams are trained by TSA's CTES. However, according to TSA officials, because of resource constraints, TSA contracted with Strijder Group K9, which subcontracted to Auburn University's Canine Detection Training Center to train some of the PSC teams.

[11] An explosive training aid is any explosive used to test and train a canine in explosives detection.

randomly selected among all the possible areas, but according to CTES, include the area that is most relevant to the type of canine team (e.g., teams assigned to airports will be evaluated in areas such as aircraft and cargo). Canine teams must find a certain percentage of the explosive training aids to pass their annual evaluation. In addition, a specified number of nonproductive responses (NPR)—when a canine responds to a location where no explosives odor is present—are allowed to pass an evaluation and maintain certification. After passing the conventional evaluation, PSC teams are required to undergo an additional annual evaluation that includes detecting explosives on a person, or being carried by a person. PSC teams are tested in different locations within the sterile areas and checkpoints of an airport.[12] A certain number of persons must be detected, and a specified number of NPRs are allowed for PSC certification.

TSA HAS TAKEN STEPS TO ANALYZE CANINE TEAM DATA TO IDENTIFY PROGRAM TRENDS

Since our January 2013 report, TSA has taken steps to analyze key data on the performance of its canine teams to better identify program trends, as we recommended. In January 2013, we reported that TSA collected and used key canine program data in its Canine Website System (CWS), a central management database, but it could better analyze these data to identify program trends. Table 2 highlights some of the key data elements included in the CWS.

TABLE 2.—EXAMPLES OF DATA ELEMENTS RECORDED IN THE CANINE WEBSITE SYSTEM (CWS)

Data Element	Description
Training minutes	Canine handlers record time spent conducting training to ensure canine teams maintain proficiency in detecting explosives odor. The Transportation Security Administration (TSA) requires canine teams to conduct a minimum of 240 proficiency training minutes every 4 weeks (month) and for handlers to record training minutes in the CWS within 48 hours.
Utilization minutes	Law enforcement officer teams record time spent patrolling transportation terminals, searching for explosives odor in rail cars and buses, for example, and screening air cargo. Transportation security inspector teams record time spent screening cargo, which is their primary responsibility. TSA requires canine handlers to record utilization minutes in CWS within 48 hours.
Certification rates	Canine Training and Evaluation Section evaluators record the results (certified [1] or decertified [2]) of annual canine team evaluations.
Short-notice assessments ...	Field canine coordinators (FCC) administer short-notice assessments—covert tests to assess canine teams' level of operational effectiveness—on two canine teams within each participating agency they oversee each year. FCCs are required to document results of short-notice assessments, and handlers are required to record results, in CWS.
Final canine responses	Canine handlers record final canine responses—instances when a canine sits, indicating to its handler that it detects explosives odor. Canine handlers are instructed to document final canine responses in CWS and submit swab samples to TSA's Canine Explosives Unit to be analyzed for explosives odor.

Source: GAO analysis of TSA documentation. GAO–14–695T

---

[12] The sterile area of an airport is the portion in an airport, defined in the airport's security program, that provides passengers access to boarding aircraft and to which the access generally is controlled by TSA through the screening of persons and property. See 49 C.F.R. § 1540.5.

In January 2013, we found that NEDCTP was using CWS data to track and monitor canine teams' performance. Specifically, field canine coordinators (FCC) reviewed CWS data to determine how many training and utilization minutes canine teams conducted on a monthly basis. NEDCTP management used CWS data to determine, for example, how many canine teams were certified in detecting explosive odors, as well as the number of teams that passed short-notice assessments. However, in our January 2013 report, we also found that TSA had not fully analyzed the performance data it collected in CWS to identify program trends and areas that were working well or in need of corrective action. For example:

- *Training minutes.*—TSA tracked the number of training minutes canine teams conducted on a monthly basis, as well as the types of explosives and search areas used when training, to ensure teams maintained their proficiency in detecting explosive training aids. However, we found that TSA did not analyze training minute data over time (from month to month) and therefore was unable to determine trends related to canine teams' compliance with the requirement. On the basis of our analysis of TSA's data, we determined that some canine teams were repeatedly not in compliance with TSA's 240-minute training requirement, in some cases for 6 months or more in a 1-year time period.
- *Utilization minutes.*—We found that TSA collected and analyzed data monthly on the amount of cargo TSI air cargo canine teams screened in accordance with the agency's requirement. However, it was unclear how the agency used this information to identify trends to guide longer-term future program efforts and activities, since our analysis of TSA's cargo screening data from September 2011 through July 2012 showed that TSI air cargo teams Nation-wide generally exceeded their monthly requirement. We concluded that TSA could increase the percentage of cargo it required TSI canine teams to screen.
- *Certification rates.*—We found that TSA tracked the number of certified and decertified canine teams, but was unable to analyze these data to identify trends in certification rates because these data were not consistently tracked and recorded prior to 2011. Specifically, we could not determine what, if any, variances existed in the certification rates among LEO and TSI teams over time because CTES reported it was unable to provide certification rates by type of canine team for calendar years 2008 through 2010. According to CTES, the agency recognized the deficiency and was in the process of implementing procedures to address data collection, tracking, and record-keeping issues.
- *Short-notice assessments (covert tests).*—We found that when TSA was performing short-notice assessments (prior to their suspension in May 2012), it was not analyzing the results beyond the pass and fail rates.[13] We concluded that without conducting the assessments and analyzing the results of these tests to determine if there were any search areas or type of explosives in which canine teams were more effective compared with others, and what, if any, training may have been needed to mitigate deficiencies, TSA was missing an opportunity to fully utilize the results.
- *Final canine responses.*—Our analysis of final canine responses and data on corresponding swab samples used to verify the presence of explosives odor revealed that canine teams were not submitting swab samples to NEDCTP's Canine Explosives Unit (CEU). Specifically, we determined that the number of swab samples sent by canine handlers to CEU for scientific review was far lower than the number of final canine responses recorded in CWS. We concluded that without the swab samples, TSA was not able to more accurately determine the extent to which canine teams were effectively detecting explosive materials in real-world scenarios.

In January 2013, we recommended that TSA regularly analyze available data to identify program trends and areas that are working well and those in need of corrective action to guide program resources and activities. These analyses could include, but not be limited to, analyzing and documenting trends in proficiency training minutes, canine utilization, results of short-notice assessments and final canine responses, performance differences between LEO and TSI canine teams, as well as an assessment of the optimum location and number of canine teams that should be deployed to secure the U.S. transportation system. TSA concurred with our recommendation and has taken actions to address it. Specifically, TSA is monitoring

---

[13] TSA suspended the short-notice assessments because of FCC staffing shortages.

canine teams' training minutes over time by producing annual reports. TSA also reinstated short notice assessments in July 2013, and in the event a team fails, the FCC completes a report that includes an analysis of the team's training records to identify an explanation for the failure. In April 2013, TSA reminded canine handlers of the requirement to submit swab samples of their canines' final responses, and reported that the number of samples submitted that same month, increased by 450 percent, when compared with sample submissions in April 2012. CEU is producing reports on the results of its analysis of the swab samples for the presence of explosives odor. In June 2014, TSA officials told us that in March 2014, NEDCTP stood up a new office, known as the Performance Measurement Section, to perform analyses of canine team data. We believe that these actions address the intent of our recommendation and could better position TSA to identify program trends to better target resources and activities based on what is working well and what may be in need of corrective action.

TSA HAS CONDUCTED ADDITIONAL PSC TEAM EFFECTIVENESS ASSESSMENTS AND DE-PLOYED SOME TEAMS TO HIGHEST-RISK AIRPORTS, BUT ADDITIONAL ACTIONS ARE NEEDED

TSA Has Conducted Additional PSC Team Effectiveness Assessments, but Has Not Compared PSC Teams With Conventional Canine Teams

In our January 2013 report, we found that TSA began deploying PSC teams in April 2011 prior to determining the teams' operational effectiveness. However, in June 2012, the DHS Science and Technology Directorate (S&T) and TSA began conducting effectiveness assessments to help demonstrate the effectiveness of PSC teams.[14] On the basis of these assessments, DHS S&T and TSA's NEDCTP recommended that the assessment team conduct additional testing and that additional training and guidance be provided to canine teams. See the hyperlink in the note for figure 2 for videos of training exercises at one airport showing instances when PSC teams detected, and failed to detect, explosives odor. In January 2013, we concluded that TSA could have benefited from completing effectiveness assessments of PSCs before deploying them on a Nation-wide basis to determine whether they are an effective method of screening passengers in the U.S. airport environment.

Figure 2: Video Stills Showing Passenger Screening Canine (PSC) Teams Training in Airport Terminal, June 2012

Source: GAO. | GAO-14-695T

Note: To view the full videos, please click on hyperlink to view Part 1 and Part 2.

We also reported in January 2013 that TSA had not completed an assessment to determine where within the airport PSC teams would be most effectively utilized, but rather TSA leadership focused on initially deploying PSC teams to a single location within the airport—the sterile area—because it thought it would be the best way to foster stakeholders', specifically airport operators' and law enforcement agencies', acceptance of the teams. Stakeholders were resistant to the deployment of PSC teams because they have civilian handlers, and TSA's response resolution protocols

---

[14] S&T is the primary research and development arm of DHS and manages science and technology research for the Department's components, such as TSA.

do not require the teams to be accompanied by a law enforcement officer.[15] According to TSA's Assistant Administrator for the Office of Security Operations, to alleviate airport stakeholders' concerns regarding TSA's response resolution protocols, the agency initially deployed PSC teams to the sterile areas, thereby enabling TSA to gather data on the value of PSC teams in the airport environment while reducing the likelihood of a final response from a PSC, since an individual has already passed through several layers of screening when entering the sterile area. However, aviation stakeholders we interviewed raised concerns about this deployment strategy, stating that PSC teams would be more effectively utilized in non-sterile areas of the airport, such as curbside or in the lobby areas. TSA subsequently deployed PSC teams to the passenger screening checkpoints. However, DHS S&T did not plan to assess the effectiveness of PSCs on the public side, beyond the checkpoint, since TSA was not planning to deploy PSCs to the public side of the airport when DHS S&T designed its test plan. In January 2013, we concluded that comprehensive effectiveness assessments that include a comparison of PSC teams in both the sterile and public areas of the airport could help TSA determine if it is beneficial to deploy PSCs to the public side of airports, in addition to or in lieu of the sterile area and checkpoint.

During the June 2012 assessment of PSC teams' effectiveness, TSA conducted one of the search exercises with three conventional canine teams. Although this assessment was not intended to be included as part of DHS S&T's and TSA's formal assessment of PSC effectiveness, the results of the assessment suggested, and TSA officials and DHS S&T's Canine Explosives Detection Project Manager agreed, that a systematic assessment of PSCs with conventional canines could provide TSA with information to determine whether PSCs provide an enhanced security benefit compared with conventional LEO aviation canine teams that have already been deployed to airport terminals. In January 2013, we concluded that an assessment would help clarify whether additional investments for PSC training are warranted. We also concluded that since PSC teams are trained in both conventional and passenger screening methods, TSA could decide to convert existing PSC teams to conventional canine teams, thereby limiting the additional resource investments associated with training and maintaining the new PSC teams.

We recommended that TSA expand and complete testing, in conjunction with DHS S&T, to assess the effectiveness of PSCs and conventional canines in all airport areas deemed appropriate prior to making additional PSC deployments to help: (1) Determine whether PSCs are effective at screening passengers, and resource expenditures for PSC training are warranted, and (2) inform decisions regarding the type of canine team to deploy and where to optimally deploy such teams within airports. TSA concurred and has taken some actions to address our recommendation, but further action is needed to fully address it. Specifically, in June 2014, TSA reported that through its PSC Focused Training and Assessment Initiative, a two-cycle assessment to establish airport-specific optimal working areas, assess team performance, and train teams on best practices, it had assessed PSC teams deployed to 27 airports cumulating in a total of 1,048 tests. On the basis of these tests, TSA determined that PSC teams are effective and should be deployed at the checkpoint queue. In February 2014, TSA launched a third PSC assessment cycle to determine how PSCs' effectiveness changes over time in order to determine their optimal duration time when working the checkpoint queue (i.e., how many minutes they can work and continue to be effective).

Although TSA has taken steps to determine whether PSC teams are effective and where in the airport environment to optimally deploy such teams, as of June 2014, TSA has not compared the effectiveness of PSCs and conventional canines in order to determine if the greater cost of training canines in the passenger screening method is warranted. According to TSA, the agency does not plan to include conventional canine teams in PSC assessments because conventional canines have not been through the process used with PSC canines to assess their temperament and behavior when working in proximity to people. While we recognize TSA's position that half of deployed conventional canines are of a breed not accepted for use in the PSC program, other conventional canines are suitable breeds, and have been paired with LEO aviation handlers working in proximity with people since they patrol airport terminals, including ticket counters and curbside areas. We continue to believe that TSA should conduct an assessment to determine whether conventional canines are as effective detecting explosives odor on passengers when compared with PSC teams

---

[15] Unlike LEOs, TSIs (PSC handlers) are unarmed civilians with no authority to take law enforcement action (e.g., arrest or detain). The response resolution protocols require the handler to be accompanied by two additional personnel that may, but not always, include a law enforcement officer.

working in the checkpoint queue. As we reported, since PSC teams are trained in both conventional and passenger screening methods, TSA could decide to convert existing PSC teams to conventional canine teams, thereby limiting the additional resource investments associated with training and maintaining PSC teams.

TSA Deployed Some PSC Teams to Highest-Risk Airports

In our January 2013 report, we found that TSA's 2012 Strategic Framework calls for the deployment of PSC teams based on risk; however, airport stakeholder concerns about the appropriateness of TSA's response resolution protocols for these teams resulted in PSC teams not being deployed to the highest-risk airports. TSA officials stated that PSC teams were not deployed to the highest-risk airports for various reasons, including concerns from an airport law enforcement association about TSA's decision to deploy PSC teams with civilian TSI handlers and the appropriateness of TSA's response resolution protocols. These protocols require the canine handler to be accompanied by two additional personnel that may, but not always, include a law enforcement officer. According to representatives from an airport law enforcement association, these protocols are not appropriate for a suicide bombing attempt requiring an immediate law enforcement response. TSA's decision to deploy PSC teams only to airports where they would be willingly accepted by stakeholders resulted in PSC teams not being deployed to the highest-risk airports on its high-risk list. Moreover, PSC teams that were deployed to high-risk airports, specifically two airports we visited, were not being used for passenger screening because TSA and the local law enforcement agencies had not reached agreement on the PSC response resolution protocols.

We recommended that if PSCs are determined to provide an enhanced security benefit, TSA should coordinate with airport stakeholders to deploy future PSC teams to the highest-risk airports, and ensure that deployed PSC teams are utilized as intended, consistent with its statutory authority to provide for the screening of passengers and their property. TSA concurred with our recommendation, and has taken action to address it. Specifically, as of June 2014, the PSC teams for which TSA had funding and not already deployed to a specific airport at the time our report was issued have been deployed to, or allocated to, the highest-risk airports. According to TSA, it was successful in deploying PSC teams to airports where they were previously declined by aviation stakeholders for various reasons. For example, TSA officials explained that stakeholders have realized that PSCs are an effective means for detecting explosives odor, and no checkpoints have closed because of a nonproductive response. PSCs also help reduce wait times at airport checkpoints because PSC teams are one method by which TSA can operate Managed Inclusion—a tool that allows passengers who have not, for example, enrolled in TSA PreCheck™ to access to PreCheck™ screening lanes.[16] According to TSA, PSC teams provide an added layer of security, making it possible for TSA to provide expedited screening to passengers who have not enrolled in TSA PreCheck™ and therefore have not had a background check.[17] In November 2013, TSA also reported it was making progress in working with stakeholders to allow PSC teams to work at checkpoints at airports where PSC teams were not previously performing passenger screening, but rather were training and screening air cargo. In June 2014, TSA officials reported that of all the airports where PSC teams had been deployed, all but one airport agreed to allow TSA to conduct screening of individuals at passenger screening checkpoint queues. We believe that these actions address the intent of our recommendation, contingent upon TSA comparing PSC teams with conventional canine teams.

Chairman Hudson, Ranking Member Richmond, and Members of the subcommittee, this completes my prepared statement. I would be happy to respond to any questions you may have at this time.

Mr. HUDSON. Thank you, Ms. Grover.
The Chairman recognizes Mr. Connell to testify.

---

[16] Through the TSA PreCheck™ program, passengers who experience expedited screening may not have to remove their shoes; may leave their liquids and gels and laptops in carry-on baggage, and are not required to divest light outerwear, jackets, or belts when passing through screening checkpoints. We have an on-going review of the TSA PreCheck™ program, including Managed Inclusion, and anticipate issuing a report in September 2014.

[17] For PreCheck™ applicants, TSA conducts a background check that includes checks against law enforcement, immigration, and intelligence databases, including a fingerprint-based criminal history records check conducted through the Federal Bureau of Investigation. The results are used by TSA to decide if an individual poses a sufficiently low-risk to transportation or National security to participate in PreCheck™.

STATEMENT OF CHRIS CONNELL, PRESIDENT, COMMODITY FORWARDERS, INC., TESTIFYING ON BEHALF OF THE AIRFORWARDERS ASSOCIATION

Mr. CONNELL. Chairman Hudson, Ranking Member Richmond, Members of the committee, thank you for hearing us on this important hearing.

My name is Chris Connell, president of Commodity Forwarders. We are a perishable specialist in the freight forwarding industry. I also serve as an elected board member for the AFA, the Airforwarders Association.

As you have heard, the AFA represents over 360 members ranging from small to large businesses, employing upwards of about 10,000 employees and subcontractors. The business models vary from domestic to world-wide operations, from air to ocean and from truck to rail.

I am helping facilitate exports, imports, and domestic moves of many products. Our members own aircraft. They work with scheduled airlines. They run aircraft cargo airplanes. Our members are key to global trade.

Safety and security is the core to our members' livelihoods. Air forwarders have worked tirelessly with Government, customers, partners to better source the global supply chain. We work due diligently on to comply with the 100 percent screening mandate from the September 11 findings.

We currently are also working with U.S. Customs and Border Patrol, TSA, and on the Air Cargo Advance Screening Pilots to move forward. We are highly aware that the threat to the aviation industry remains high, and we are determined to do our part to ensure safety.

Canines have long proven to be an effective security tool for TSA and many of the agencies. In the wake of the 9/11 Commission recommendations that was passed in 2007, TSA created the Certified Cargo Screening Program, CCSP, which permitted certified freight companies to screen cargo away from the airport.

This legislation allowed screening to be performed through a variety of methods, physical inspection, X-ray, explosive trace detection technology. Using specifically-trained dogs was deemed to be an acceptable way to screen cargo, but was restricted for the CCSP program.

AFP believes that privatized canines can be a potentially valuable part to a multiple layered approach, another tool in the toolbox, if you will, for CCSFs to perform their process. Privatized canines are not the magic bullet when it comes to screening. There is really no magic bullet at this point.

Our belief is that the industry—our belief as an industry association is that the best route to the highest level of safety and security is through the multi-layered risk-based approach that uses the best possible tools available. Only the sums of those parts equal a more secure supply chain.

The TSA has approved the use of dogs, and only on airports. TSA-owned canines are limited in number busier airport passenger terminals, and shared with airline cargo facilities with tarmac access. For hundreds of forwarders and shippers who operate off-airport CCSFs, there really is no option to use canines at their premises.

The issue as we see it is whether authorizing private companies to provide dogs to conduct security screening at Government-certified freight forwarding facilities, assuming those dogs are trained and certified to Government standards, is a good thing to do moving forward. We believe that is something the TSA should move forward with hand-in-hand with industry.

Just this month the AFA surveyed our members and found that three-quarters of our respondents, half of them which are CCSFs, say that it would strongly consider using dogs provided by private companies if they were given the option. Companies such as Atlas, DHS, FedEx, UPS, TNT are highly supportive of having the option to use privatized canines to screen cargo.

In 2013 my Los Angeles facility screened over 6.7 million packages through a combination of ETD, X-ray, and metal detection. Due to the density of produce, seafood, and proteins, the majority of the screening, if not all, was done by at the box level.

We have not seen an economically feasible technology to date to screen high-density cargo by the skid. It seems to be nothing in the pipeline. That is why we would like TSA to consider using dogs for the cargo CCSF program.

The products my customers ship are items that families eat every day and need cool chain. Food safety and other areas for efficient transportation methods are key to not just food safety, but also the security and the efficiencies of the businesses we run.

CFI spent $1.6 million on screeners, loaders, and forklift drivers to screen those 6.7 million cases. Now keep in mind, that is just in our Los Angeles facility alone, for a small to medium-sized forwarder.

Our customers range from Costco, Wal-Mart, Tyson, Cisco, and many other small to medium-sized businesses. They are looking for the least traumatic screening method as possible, not just to control costs, but also to maintain the best quality of food we ship and people eat.

Time is money in our business. Accordingly, we are highly interested in any solution that can help us expedite the screening process, move our perishables more quickly through the supply chain and still provide the utmost in food safety and security. We think dogs can really help us do that, again, not as a magic bullet, but as an important option to give us more tools in the toolbox, so to speak.

We believe that companies like a CFI have saved—can save over a $1 million a year at a single facility if we access to third-party solution deploying canines. Of course our customers would highly appreciate the time, savings, and the solutions to help achieve this.

It is my understanding that in 2011 the TSA ran a pilot program to test the feasibility of implementing a third-party explosive detection canine program that would make explosive detection dogs available to screen all cargo before it goes to a passenger or a cargo aircraft. We also understand that while those results were mixed, but offered encouragement that private-sector canines could meet TSA standards.

I would hope that the lessons learned by the TSA and the private canine companies to jointly build testing criteria for testing not just the private but also the Government dogs as a benchmark would be useful in the next phase.

Given the track record of canines in cargo screening, proceeding with the private-sector option with solutions fully regulated, certified, and monitored by TSA would square with the screening approaches under CCSF, such as in-house X-ray, ETD where the Government does not develop the technology and solutions in-house, rather relies on private sector to do the work and puts it through a rigid testing before authorizing it for use.

We think this approach would work well for using dogs just as it did for X-ray and other technologies in the pipeline.

In conclusion, we urge that the TSA gets funding to help finalize its efforts to develop a certification program for private companies to enable them to use their own canines, certified to TSA standards, to meet Federal air cargo screening mandates through the CCSF program. Leveraging private-sector resources will introduce much-needed additional canines to the cargo screening system.

The Aviation Security Advisory Committee, ASAC, comprised of stakeholders, including the Airforwarders Association, as diverse as the Association of Flight Attendants to the Pan Am 103 survivors, have endorsed the concept of private screening through canines. It is our hope that this hearing will spur what appears to be a near-universal support for private canines.

Thank you for your opportunity. I will be happy to answer questions as you deem fit.

[The prepared statement of Mr. Connell follows:]

PREPARED STATEMENT OF CHRIS CONNELL

JUNE 24, 2014

Chairman Hudson, Ranking Member Richmond, and Members of the committee, thank you for holding this important hearing and for inviting me to testify.

My name is Chris Connell and I am the president of Commodity Forwarders, a freight forwarding company specializing in perishable products. We are headquartered in Los Angeles and we operate both domestically and internationally. Today I am testifying on behalf of the Airforwarders Association (AfA), on whose board I sit.

The Airforwarders Association represents 360 member companies that together employ tens of thousands of employees and contractors. AfA members range from small businesses to large companies with thousands of employees, and with business models varying from domestic to world-wide operations. Some of our members operate their own aircraft, but most use scheduled airlines and operators of cargo planes to move the freight they are handling.

Accordingly, we move our clients' cargo throughout the supply chain in the most timely and cost-efficient manner, whether it is carried on aircraft, truck, rail, or ship. As many of our members operate internationally, we are a key cog in global trade and logistics.

CARGO SCREENING

Safety and security are at the core of our members' livelihoods. Since our Nation and our aviation industry came under attack on September 11, 2001, air freight forwarders have worked tirelessly with our Government, our customers, and our airline partners to better secure the global supply chain. AfA members have worked diligently to comply with the 100% cargo screening mandate and we are currently working with U.S. Customs and Border Protection (CBP) and the Transportation Security Administration (TSA) on the Air Cargo Advanced Screening (ACAS) pilots. We are highly aware that the threat to the aviation industry remains high, and we are determined to do our part to ensure safety.

Given the topic for today's hearing, I will say, in the spirit of full disclosure, that in addition to freight forwarders, the Airforwarders Association also consists of air cargo screening technology companies and canine screening companies. But I am not going to tell you that privatized canines are a magic bullet when it comes to screening, because that would not square with our belief as an industry association that the best route to the highest level of safety and security is through a multi-layer, risk-based approach.

Accordingly, what I am here to state is our belief that privatized canines can be a potentially valuable part of this multi-layer approach—another important tool in the toolbox, if you will—that also includes a range of other technology solutions and Government-trained canines for our members to utilize to meet screening requirements.

The issue here, as we see it, is whether authorizing private companies to provide dogs to conduct security screening at Government-certified freight forwarding facilities—assuming those dogs are trained and certified to Government standards—is a good thing to do. We believe that it is something that TSA should move forward with.

As you are aware, canines have long proven to be an effective security tool. In the wake of the 9/11 Commission Recommendations Act that was passed by Congress in 2007, TSA created the Certified Cargo Screening Program (CCSP), which permitted certified freight companies to screen cargo away from the airport. The legislation also allowed screening to be performed through a variety of methods including physical inspection, X-ray, and explosive trace detection technology. Use of specially trained dogs was deemed as an acceptable way to screen air cargo.

Unfortunately, TSA has permitted only the use of its own dogs, and only at the airport. TSA-owned canines are limited in number, busy at airport passenger terminals and are shared with airline freight facilities only as time and availability permit. So, for the hundreds of forwarders who operate off-airport Certified Cargo Screening Facilities (CCSF), there really is no option to use dogs on their premises.

Just this month we surveyed our members and found that fully three-quarters of the respondents—about half of whom operate CCSFs—say they would strongly consider using dogs provided by private companies if they were given the option to do that. Additionally, I know that Atlas, DHL, Fedex, UPS, and TNT are highly supportive of having the option to use privatized canines to screen cargo.

Let me tell you about my own company's experience in operating a CCSF.

In 2013, CFI's Los Angeles facility screened just over 6.7 million packages through a combination of ETD, X-ray, and metal detection. Due to the density of the produce, seafood, and proteins we move, most of the screening is done at the box level. Cold chain is another area that requires a more efficient method of screening. CFI spent about $1.6 million on screeners, loaders, and fork-lift drivers to screen most of those 6.7 million cases. Companies such as Costco, Walmart, Tyson, Kuehne and Nagel and Sysco, are asking CFI for the least adverse screening method as possible, not just to control cost but to best maintain the quality of the food we ship and people eat.

Accordingly, we are highly interested in any solution that can help us expedite the screening process, move our perishables more quickly through the supply chain, and still provide the utmost in safety and security of what we ship. We think dogs can really help us do that—again, not as a magic bullet, but as an important option to help get the most out of the other solutions we are already using.

Time is money in our business. And right now we believe that we could save over a million dollars a year at our LAX facility if we had access to a third-party solution deploying canines. Of course our customers would highly appreciate the time savings that this solution would help us achieve.

PAST TESTING OF PRIVATIZED DOGS

I understand that in 2011, TSA ran a pilot program to test the feasibility of implementing a third-party private explosive detection canine program that would make explosive detection dogs available to screen all cargo before it goes on passenger and all-cargo aircraft. I also understand that while the results were mixed, they offered encouragement that private-sector canines could meet TSA standards. I would hope that the lessons learned by the canine companies will be useful should you conduct further testing.

I would add that, given the track record of canines in cargo screening, proceeding with a private-sector option—with solutions fully regulated, certified, and monitored by Government agencies—would square with other screening approaches such as in-house X-ray and ETD, where the Government does not develop the technologies and solutions in-house. Rather, it relies on the private sector to do this work and then puts it through rigid testing before authorizing it for use. We think this approach would work well for using dogs.

CONCLUSION

In conclusion, we urge TSA to finalize its efforts to develop a certification program for private companies to enable them to use their own canines, certified to TSA standards, to meet Federal air cargo screening mandates. Leveraging private-sector resources will introduce much-needed additional canines into the cargo screening system. The Aviation Security Advisory Committee (ASAC) comprised of stake-holders, including the Airforwarders Association and as diverse as the Association of Flight Attendants to the Pan Am 103 survivors have endorsed the concept of privatized screening. It is our hope that this hearing will spur what appears to be near-universal support for privatized canines.

Thank you for this opportunity and I will be happy to answer any questions that you may have.

Mr. HUDSON. Thank you, Mr. Connell. I apologize for mispronouncing your name. One of my favorite bands in high school was the Connells from Raleigh, NC and I can't help it.

Mr. CONNELL. It happens all the time.

Mr. HUDSON. So sorry about that. But thank you to all the witnesses.

Before I begin my question I ask unanimous consent to insert a statement by K2 Solutions into the record, supporting the use of canine teams in explosive detection.

Without objection, so ordered.

[The information follows:]

STATEMENT OF K2 SOLUTIONS, INC.

Chairman Hudson, Ranking Member Richmond, and distinguished Members of the subcommittee: Thank you for the opportunity to present written testimony advocating for the effective utilization of canine teams in support of the United States' on-going efforts to improve and advance security measures. As president and chief operations officer of K2 Solutions, Inc., it is my distinct honor and privilege to present a corporate perspective, derived from extensive experience in the canine industry, in an effort to aid Nation-wide efforts geared toward effective and efficient explosives detection and mitigation of related threats.

The unparalleled efficacy of explosives detection canines has been supported and acknowledged by research scientists, Government officials, and politicians alike; by military advisors holding some of the highest-ranking positions within the Department of Defense; as well as soldiers in the ground forces who lived to tell stories of the dogs that saved their lives. It takes little effort to find quotes from high-ranking military officials touting canines as invaluable assets aiding in securing the protection of our troops in combat and the safety of our citizens at home. In his Memoirs, Robert M. Gates remarked, "for all the technology, there was common agreement that one sensor worked better at detecting IEDs than anything else: a dog's nose." General Colin Powell has stated, "war dogs have, indeed, served the nation well and saved many lives. Dogs continue to serve to protect Americans both in combat zones and in homeland security roles." General David Petraeus remarked, "the capability they (Military Working Dogs) bring to the fight cannot be replicated by man or machine. By all measures of performance their yield outperforms any asset we have in our inventory. Our Army (and military) would be remiss if we failed to invest more in this incredibly valuable resource."

Even more prevalent are the stories of marines and soldiers who were supported by explosives detection canines in war zones and on the battlefield. These testimonials have a distinctly different tone than other canine-related accolades; the technical proficiency of the canine is embodied in the personal accounts as told by the men and women to whom these dogs were true partners. The following is a mere glimpse of the value of canine detection from the perspective of those standing on the front lines.

Lance Cpl. Jarrett Hatley: "My dog Blue is pretty much like another Marine, I guess. He doesn't know he's doing it, but he's protecting all of us. If I have him on a patrol and there's an IED that could hurt us, I know he'll find it."

Sgt. 1st Class Regina Johnson: "There's no doubt about my dog: Number one, he will protect me. Number two, he will find a bomb."

Staff Sgt. Robert Calhoun (following the unexpected death of his MWD, Rony): "All I ever wanted was to save lives and contribute to the mission success. Rony saved lives. Rony saved my life when we went into an abandoned compound, and he found a 155-pound before I stepped on the pressure plate. Before we left, we were awarded the Bronze Star. He's the reason—he brought us home."

While the nature of the commendation may vary depending on the source, there is unwavering support for the the utilization of canines in explosives detection and threat mitigation, which steadfastly remains one of the most valuable capabilities in our arsenal.

Between 2004 and 2010, HEDDO spent approximately $19 billion researching and developing advanced technologies in an effort to produce equipment that could match the detection capabilities of a dog while being maintained at a lower cost. On June 20, 2010, Lieutenant General Michael Oates, then commander of the Joint Improvised Explosive Device Defeat Organization, told a conference, quite simply, that "dogs are the best detectors." Since that time, there have been no marked changes or advancements in detection technology; and to date, there exists no technology that can remotely rival the accuracy and efficiency of canines in the field of explosives detection.

The time and money that has been spent by the U.S. Government in an attempt to solve a problem for which an obvious, efficient, and cost-effective solution already exists has not gone unnoticed by the media nor by the taxpayers at large. While there is no question that technology plays an integral role in our Nation's overall advancement and is the driving force behind much of our success in developing and instituting state-of-the-art security measures both overseas and at home, it is imperative that the Congress recognize the value of utilizing canines for explosives detection—a technology that despite years of research and billions of dollars in investments remains unsurpassed.

The utility of deploying canines as a security measure for the purpose of detecting explosives and mitigating related threats is incontrovertible. However, the degree of accuracy and consistency with which canines detect explosives and other hazardous materials is largely dependent upon the methodologies employed during training. As a result, substantial consideration should be given when determining whether Government and non-Government security agencies are adequately equipped to facilitate and maintain every aspect of a canine program internally—from initial training, to certification, to on-going sustainment training required for long-term effectiveness. While agencies such as the TSA have seen some success as a result of internal canine programs established to bolster transportation security, the GAO has pointed out that reports compiled on such internal-agency canine programs indicate areas of weakness such as inaccurate or inconsistent detection rates, insufficiencies in the training of both the canine and handler, and the credibility of internal evaluations and certifications of canine teams.

By partnering with third-party providers such as K2, the TSA and Government security agencies will be positioned to take advantage of methodologies and training tactics that have proven successful in establishing effective canine detection programs for the Military, DoD, and local and Federal law enforcement agencies alike. Much of K2's success is a result of the company's focus on three essential areas of practice: Comprehensive analyses of programs and training initiatives, including follow-on training; continuous support and facilitation of research and development; and formulation and use of innovative technologies and services, such as explosive detection solutions that provide safe stand-off distance to personnel using the technology.

Through the utilization of third-party vendors, the Government realizes the benefits of established techniques and procedures; this starts with the assessment and selection of quality canines. To date, K2 has successfully procured, trained, and assessed over 1,570 canines, and provided certifications and re-certifications for more than 800 explosive-odor and narcotic-detection canines to military, law enforcement, and civilian clients around the world. This includes six major contract awards in support of the Marine Corps' Improvised Explosive Device Detector Dog (IDD) Program, U.S. Special Operations Command (USSOCOM), and the British Military Working Dog Program.

Explosive detection teams can provide invaluable security support to transportation and security agencies when equipped with the proper initial training and requisite follow-on training. Advanced canine explosives detection teams are among the most effective in countering threats posed by IEDs and require more specialized training than the traditional detection canine, and such training is every bit as essential for the handler as it is for the canine. For instance, K2's Person-Borne Explosives Detection Dog (PBEDD) Teams have not only the ability to consistently detect person-borne explosives present in average amounts, but also to alert with remarkable accuracy on even trace amounts of odors. That said, even a canine team trained to the highest degree of excellence cannot be expected to maintain such rates of success in the absence of follow-on training. Because K2 views the canine team as a partnership, training is a team requirement; thus, training is always provided to the canine and the handler concurrently. By electing to out-source all or portions of the initial training, follow-on training, and/or advanced training to third-party experts, agencies will see marked increases in the consistency and overall success of explosive detection canine programs.

An additional point worthy of note is the fact that agencies such as the TSA currently conduct evaluations and certifications in-house. While internal evaluations can be constructive if carried out regularly and uniformly, agencies would realize a greater benefit by engaging external sources to administer at least some percentage of the evaluations. The use of external evaluation teams has proven highly effective in providing consistent and objective results. Under a contract with Johns Hopkins University, K2 executed initial training using in-house resources available at the K2 K9 training facility, followed by intensive on-site training, to provide the University of Maryland with canines capable of detecting person-borne explosives in a matter of 14 weeks. This type of detection capability is very similar to the type of detection for which the TSA Passenger Screening Canines (PSCs) are intended. Because canine detection of person-borne explosives is a relatively new technology, it was imperative to seek external certifications to ensure objectivity and credibility. One of the main reasons this program has been so effective is that the International Police Work Dog Association (IPWDA) was engaged to objectively provide the certifications for the University of Maryland Program. It is worthy to note that the outcome of the certification was a 100 percent rate of passage, and the canines in the program have continued to exceed expectations. Regular testing and evaluation by an accredited objective entity such as the IPWDA is a critical component of any successful canine program.

In the last 2 years, K2 has successfully supplied third-party certified handler teams to perform detection searches at a multitude of different sporting and recreational venues for security enhancement and has received positive feedback from clients across the board. Commercial vendors have found this type of relationship to be advantageous in that the client's objectives are satisfied without having to support canine kenneling, sustainment, and training exercises in-house. K2 ensures that its canines are constantly trained to detect newly developed threat odors and requires all in-house trained canine teams to be certified externally to ensure the canine teams' capability is evaluated in an objective manner. While outsourcing can be extraordinarily beneficial, the advantages are recognized fully only through the use of qualified third-party vendors.

Over the past decade, the United States has spent significant resources, and born considerable sacrifice in developing battle-proven, highly-effective canine detection capabilities. One of the great benefits resulting from this effort is a clear template showing what works and what does not when it comes to optimizing canine detection programs. As our Nation shifts focus from theatres of operation to greater protection of the homeland against a wide array of threats, it is imperative that we recognize the necessity of using capabilities and methodologies that have seen consistent success in IED detection and related threat mitigation. In order to achieve optimum results, greater emphasis must be placed on the importance of Governmental and non-Governmental agencies establishing partnerships and alliances with third-party providers that have a proven track record of success in the field of advanced canine explosive training and detection.

Mr. HUDSON. I will now recognize myself for 5 minutes to ask questions.

I will start off just sort-of with a general question for everybody. I am obviously a strong proponent of a risk-based multi-layered approach to security. Having said that, I believe that canines are a highly effective, efficient, less-invasive tool than most of the technologies designed to detect explosives.

I would like to hear from each of you. What qualities or capabilities, from your perspective, set canines apart from other explosive detection technologies that we can deploy at airports with passengers?

So maybe we just go in the order of testimony.

Ms. HARVEY. Yes, sir. There are several qualities that separate canines from other explosive detection capabilities.

At the airports the other primary technology that we use is explosive trace detection or ETDS. Canines are distinct from them in that they—the team provides a very visible deterrent. An officer or a TSI with a canine, there is no question that that is a deterrent to our adversaries.

The second thing is it is very portable. So while an ETD or other equipment needs to be plugged in. It is very difficult to move from place to place. The team can go wherever the mission needs.

The third thing is it is very highly effective detection capability. Along with that comes care and feeding of the team. So while an ETD has to be plugged in and isn't as portable, it is available 24/7.

So they are all important parts of TSA's multi-layered system. Thank you, sir.

Mr. HUDSON. Thank you.

Ms. LONTZ. Just to add onto what Ms. Harvey just said, I think it is reflective of how the canines can adapt so quickly as a threat evolves. Our philosophy for training our canines is for them to train in the environment in which they work.

So our focus really is to ensure that they are the most capable asset that our canines are able to work in the multi-modal transportation venues. So we are convinced that our training process does just that, and allows us to have a very adaptable canine program that can be utilized wherever necessary.

Ms. GROVER. My comment echoes much of what you have heard before, that what we have heard from TSA is that they value the canines as a very mobile screening tool that allows the agency greater flexibility to meet their needs. And that they also value them as one of the multiple layers of security.

Mr. CONNELL. I guess, why canines? I would probably, you know, want to answer that question from another side.

The issues we see with ETD, X-ray, and metal detection is the labor intensity that needs to go into to handle skids of product at the same level, be it not just produce, seafood needs, but also hard cargo, metal, things from Caterpillar, for example, or other items of such.

We are finding that the high labor that needs to go into segregating these products to get them through at the piece level handles—creates overhead costs of not just manpower, inefficiencies of facility flow, you know log jams and getting cargo through to the airport. But the industry has managed to make due, if you will, to achieve cargo security through the layered approach.

We feel dogs bring the ability to create more of an economy of scale through a set facility, allow us to kind of deploy manpower resources better through the supply chain, and at that point do it just better, you know where it is a better result versus a human interaction saying yes or no. I hope that answers your questions.

Mr. HUDSON. That is good. To build on that, you mentioned in your testimony that your company could save over a million dollars every year if it was able to use third-party canines to conduct primary screening. I guess some of these things you mentioned are ways you would do that, some of the efficiencies you could find not having to unpack everything and run it through.

But what sort of challenges, though, on the other hand, do you currently encounter by using existing screening technologies other than—maybe you could expound on what you were saying that you—and how would that work with canines versus how it works now? Maybe you could get us a little deeper into your experience there.

Mr. CONNELL. Yes. I would say our experience, as example you bring in a skid of cherries. We owe 80 cases. Well, every one of those 80 cases have to be run separately through a machine similar to bags. There is obviously the manpower to do that, the timing, keeping it within the cool chain for better quality arrival.

Mr. HUDSON. If I can interrupt, what size machine are you running them through?

Mr. CONNELL. We are running them through—we actually had a skidded X-ray—or a skidded metal detector at one point, but the technology was not good enough to see the middle of the skid. So we deemed that technology—it is available for other cargos, not available to many different types of cargo including produce. There is too much water and too much density through the product.

So then we had to break that down and put it through really almost a machine that is similar to the bags where it is a small machine, we are putting it right through and we are putting 80 single cases through that facility through that one machine.

We found out things of such where there was not just the issue of timing and manpower and having to do this in a refrigerated environment or breaking the refrigerated environment that hurts the value of this produce, for example.

We also found out that the actual physical of moving cases and lumping them from place to place to place, skid, to machine, back onto a skid, for example, created you know a fracturing of the product and actually created product quality issues for many of our growers.

So that is just one example. There is an unforeseen quality hit that would occur when screening it this way. Compared to you know other countries who screen—because we compete in the global environment. Canada has picked cherries, things of that nature.

I would say that is probably the No. 1 issue we saw through that throughput, also the ability to handle spikes in volume. It is an agricultural product. So we have to go in and ensure and on where we can triple our volume in a single day, stacking for that, making sure you can manage that, preventing backlogs, making airplanes. Just being efficient.

We are not talking about efficiency, just purely to put in our pockets. It is also efficiency that allows us to move more cargo, gives us an economy of scale, helps our airline vendors and also allows the customers to have a better consumer price at the end either coming into or out of the United States.

Mr. HUDSON. Great. Thank you. My time is expired. So I will now recognize the Ranking Minority Member of the subcommittee, the gentleman from Louisiana, Mr. Richmond, for any questions he may have.

Mr. RICHMOND. Thank you, Mr. Chairman.

I will start with you, Ms. Grover. In your written—in your prepared remarks you mentioned that TSA has improved its analysis of canine program data relative to what you all found in 2013. Is TSA doing enough data analysis to keep track of how well the program is working?

Ms. GROVER. Yes, sir. They have made significant improvements during this past year. Perhaps most importantly is the staffing of their new Performance Measurements Office that is designed specifically to review the canine team program data.

In addition, they have taken several steps to address specific issues that we raised in our report such as they are now tracking compliance with the training minute requirement over time rather than just month-to-month. They are also doing much more detailed analysis of the reasons for the teams that fail the short notice assessments, you know the covert testing.

So as long as they continue to maintain the level of analysis that is currently in place and currently planned, and then take steps as required to address the findings, then they should be in good shape for robust oversight of the program.

Mr. RICHMOND. Thank you.

Ms. Lontz and Ms. Harvey, the 2013 report highlighted the concerns of various aviation industry stakeholders regarding the deployment of PSC teams, specifically those representing the law enforcement community. Three questions from that.

How does TSA work to mitigate stakeholders' concerns regarding the deployment of PSC teams? Are they supportive of TSA's efforts to deploy the teams as part of Managed Inclusion? Has the law enforcement community expressed concerns regarding the further expansion of the use of PSC teams in the airport?

Ms. HARVEY. Thank you, sir. TSA has taken several steps to address stakeholder concerns.

When we originally rolled out the PSC teams the concerns from our stakeholders were that there were going to be excessive hits, for lack of a better word, of the teams, and they would close down checkpoints or parts of the airport and you know cause excessive wait times for passengers.

As they have rolled out that has turned out not to be the case. We have an average of 6 to 8 responses across the country every week. I think there has only been one shut-down since the start of the program, and that was over 2 years ago.

So our approach to rolling out the teams has been to work very closely with the airports, with the airport operators, as well as the law enforcement at those airports to ensure they understand our CONOPS and what resolution procedures are going to be available and if in fact there is a hit.

You asked specifically about their use in Managed Inclusion and any law enforcement concerns. Again when we rolled out the program there were some concerns from the law enforcement community about the resolution procedures. The way that we use the teams at the checkpoint there are all of the technologies at the checkpoint to resolve any alarms that the PSCs have in the queue, and so most of those concerns have been alleviated.

Your final question is whether concerns remain with law enforcement over expansion of the program. Again, there are still, I am sure, some concerns, not so much about expansion, but again in understanding the resolution procedures that are used when there is a response of the canine team.

Thank you.

Mr. RICHMOND. Mr. Connell, in your prepared testimony you cite the expense associated with screening cargo at the box level. Is— a million dollars is what you think you all would save using a third-party canine team?

Mr. CONNELL. Canine teams have not established there is that pricing yet because they don't—they cannot tell us what their whole processes will be from the TSA. But our estimate is assuming there will be some cost coming in that about a million could be saved, you know $800,000 to $1 million could be saved just in that facility alone.

Not just to mention the through-put that comes out on quality of product and other you know unattainable—unachievable items that are hard to really describe.

Mr. RICHMOND. Have you had a chance to talk about your industry and your view with—concerning third-party canine screening with TSA? If so, has TSA been receptive?

Mr. CONNELL. We have not had—originally when CCSF came up we had light discussions about the idea of canines. But—and basically there was a huge mountain of stuff to get through, so to speak, so that probably fell to the bottom.

Since then the general questions we have had multiple years ago have been that it was just not going to happen. So we basically focused on other things that were more achievable.

I have talked to some of my competitors and some of the industry people who have said they really had the same thing, they just gave up on having the conversation because the few times it came up it never really got anywhere, for all the wrong or right reasons, budgetary, et cetera, had to go through protocols.

So we were in a way basically discouraged from having more discussions because why waste our time?

Mr. RICHMOND. I see my time is expired, but just one last quick question. We have heard all the good stuff and everybody supports it. Anyone in your industry opposed to it? If so, who?

Mr. CONNELL. You know I would say everyone is encouraged by the idea of it. We obviously have to get through a cost analysis, a detailed drill-down of what is required and things of that nature.

I would say you know maybe an average Joe, people, you know the technology companies who do X-rays and metal detection might not be the most positive on this. But again, it is a layered approach. We have to have all those tools in the bucket per se.

But from talking to the AFA respondents, talking to people, competitors, people in the industry, I have not seen any negative pushback from people who actually physically handle the cargo.

Mr. HUDSON. Thank you, Mr. Richmond.

Chairman will now recognize other Members of the committee for questions they wish to ask the witnesses. In accordance with our committee rules and practice I plan to recognize Members who were present at the start of the hearing by seniority on the subcommittee. Those coming in later will be recognized in the order of arrival.

Next I will recognize the gentleman from Alabama, Mr. Rogers, for any questions he may have.

Mr. ROGERS. Thank you, Mr. Chairman. This has been very encouraging. As you all know I have been working on this for many, many years and can talk about this subject until you get glass-eyed.

So I am thrilled to hear you all are embracing the efficacy of these explosive detection canines. I think you would agree with me that they are the most effective tool that we have. There is nothing that compares to the efficacy of these canines, particularly the explosive—the vapor wake canines in detecting explosives.

But the purpose of this hearing is to try to figure out why we haven't gotten more private third-party providers because obviously TSA can only grow so far with their canine breeding and training programs can only grow so far so fast.

So let me ask, and this would be for Ms. Harvey or Ms. Lontz, how many of the Category X airports now have explosive detection canines deployed?

Ms. HARVEY. Sir, every CAT X airport and all CAT 1 airports with the exception of four have some sort of explosive detection canine capability, whether it is led by the State and local law enforcement or TSA.

Mr. ROGERS. Do you know of those how many are vapor wake canines?

Ms. HARVEY. So we are authorized for 144 passenger screening canine, which is a little bit distinct from the vapor wake, but the same concept. Those are currently allocated to 36 airports.

Mr. ROGERS. Okay. Do you know if most of the passengers are screened by those canines as they go through the security systems?

Ms. HARVEY. So that is something that distinguishes a PSC from the technology, to the question that was asked earlier. If the passenger screening team is there and depending on the configuration of the queue, the PSC team can screen every passenger that goes through the checkpoint when they are present.

Mr. ROGERS. What about if somebody leaves a bag in the airport? Let's just say it is an absent-minded traveler who left their bag outside the restroom, goes to the terminal, 20 minutes later realizes it is missing and goes back. But in the mean time it has been reported.

When the security personnel are deployed to that bag, what is—is a canine part of that deployment to determine whether or not there are explosives in it? Or how do they approach that bag?

Ms. HARVEY. So in general the airport law enforcement are the officials who respond to those. If there are canine available, yes, many times they ask for that support.

Mr. ROGERS. Absent a canine what happens?

Ms. HARVEY. They follow their agency's protocols.

Mr. ROGERS. Which would be?

Ms. HARVEY. I am not familiar with every—with the law enforcement protocols.

Mr. ROGERS. Well let me ask, clearly you all have embraced this. What is impeding you putting more of these canines into more of the airports beyond the Category X? I would imagine in the Category X airports you don't have 24-hour or multi-shift coverage.

Ms. HARVEY. Yes. So it depends on the airport the number of teams that we have. There are some airports that have a large number, again adding up the TSA-led teams with the law enforcement teams.

We have allocated the teams that we have. Our numbers have grown significantly over the past few years, as somebody mentioned has doubled since the early 2000s. The only—right now the only hold-up on deploying more teams would be our capacity to train the teams and get them certified.

Mr. ROGERS. Well, I agree. Trust me, I know why it took so long. I have been pushing it for the last 10 years.

But my question is—I fully appreciate the limit on the capacity of what you can do in training and your own. But there are third parties out there who can do the same training that meets your standards. Why aren't we seeing those private providers utilized more? Because the Defense Department has been doing this for years. Why aren't you all using the private folks more?

This may be for Ms. Lontz. I don't—it doesn't——

Ms. HARVEY. Are you asking why we aren't using those to train the teams, the private providers?

Mr. ROGERS. To get them in airports. There are private folks that do exactly what you are doing inside your own program to breed appropriate bloodlines, train them up, to certify them, and then deploy them, just like you do. Why aren't we seeing those people used to supplement what you are doing to cover additional airports, bus stations, train stations, and whatever?

Ms. LONTZ. Certainly. So this is one of those outstanding questions that in addition to our resource concerns that the exact nature of TSA's role in the training, and in certifying and maintaining the oversight and the proficiency that would need to be worked out.

Mr. ROGERS. What kind of time line do you think that is going to work out?

Ms. HARVEY. So, we have—to summarize, in 2011 we did the pilot. While the results were somewhat promising, there were two providers. One of them provided teams that could, we believe, meet TSA standards. The other provider did not. It went through I think two canine providers and couldn't pass the basic code of recognition test.

After that to test the interest from industry sort-of fell away while they were focused on what technology they could use to meet the 100 percent mandate. Since that time we have been busy rolling out the passenger screening canine teams.

Given that there is renewed interest from industry, we are going to take a look at those concepts, at the third-party canine concept.

Mr. ROGERS. Unfortunately my time is expired. I yield back.

Mr. HUDSON. Thank the gentleman.

I recognize the gentlelady from Indiana, Mrs. Brooks, for any questions she may have.

Mrs. BROOKS. Thank you, Mr. Chairman. I would like to just continue that line of questioning that my colleague just had because that is actually the area that I was really quite interested in because we certainly know that whenever we as—now as a new

Member of Congress, we are traveling through more airports and more train stations than ever before, and bus stations.

There is a level of great comfort actually when you see a canine team there. But yet I am very familiar, having worked in law enforcement, that they only have a period of time that they can work every day because then they fatigue and they are not as effective.

So going to what gentleman from Alabama's point is, is certainly there must be a number of canine providers in the industry that are interested. If the pilot only involved two different providers, how many providers are there? I would ask you know the whole panel, that are interested in participating and then you know increasing this public-private partnership? That is essentially what it would be, would be a public-private partnership.

I appreciate that you would need to you know make sure that they meet your level of training. But how many different groups are out there that would be interested, if you know, or that you are working with? Two seems just unbelievable to me.

Ms. HARVEY. So the two that were—the two that participated in the pilot were carriers. They contracted out with canine providers. I don't know how many canine providers there are in the industry.

Mrs. BROOKS. Does anyone have any idea how many canine providers there might be who might be willing to supplement TSA's efforts?

Ms. GROVER. No, I don't. GAO hasn't looked at that specific issue.

Mr. CONNELL. I am not familiar with the exact count. I know in our research we definitely saw three that in particular were interested. I know there is a whole host of others that have been discouraged through what they feel a lackadaisical approach of testing standards, the ability to benchmark against current TSA dogs and how that translates to test criteria. But we can continue to vet them.

But I know there were some questions on, you know, is it worth their while type of thing. I think that is what is important to kind-of get established, you know the testing criteria, before you can bring more member canine units in.

Mrs. BROOKS. Would you agree, however, Mr. Connell, that there could be, as you have said, significant savings if we could supplement the number of canine teams that we had, and we ought to be encouraging the industry, those that are, you know, training the canines, that we really ought to have a huge push on this because of the savings that could really benefit your industry?

Mr. CONNELL. Yes, I would totally agree. Time is money. But also is a point where you know companies want—they were willing to fill a gap if the business model is there. I think the ability to know that is an achievable business model will definitely generate interest among many dog providers to provide so, if not necessarily from public or from private funds.

Mrs. BROOKS. Ms. Lontz, the other Federal agencies use canine teams, whether it is nuclear power plants, United States, our military personnel. Are you familiar, are they using third-party canine providers? What have any of the lessons been from other agencies that TSA maybe has explored?

Ms. LONTZ. I am sorry. I am not familiar with what the other agencies are utilizing and if they are using a third-party canine. We could certainly explore that though.

Mrs. BROOKS. Is anyone else aware whether or not other Federal agencies are using any third-party providers? Okay.

I certainly hope that we do explore that because I think that it is an incredible tool that we need to add and expand on. I have got to believe that those in the canine industry and who raise these types of incredible dogs would be very willing and would love to probably get involved in this type of work. So I just want to thank you for your work on behalf of keeping us all safe. Thank you.

Mr. HUDSON. Well, thank you. I think there is enough interest if the witnesses are willing to stick around a little bit longer, maybe we will get through another round. If that is—I don't see any no—we will try to keep it fairly brief. But this is a great discussion. I appreciate the witnesses' indulgence.

I will recognize myself for 5 minutes, but I won't take all that time. But one of the issues I was really surprised to learn is that there are four separate offices within TSA that handle canines.

Ms. Harvey and Ms. Lontz, maybe you could help me understand why. What are the different responsibilities? Why do we have four different offices that sort of all deal with one—with the canine issue?

Ms. HARVEY. Sir, a few years ago actually TSA combined the entire canine program into the Office of Security Operations, which is the organization that I work for. Ms. Lontz's organization provides the—they procure the canine, train the canines, and then provide certification of the program. But there are only two offices in TSA that lead the program.

Mr. HUDSON. Good. Well, that is—that was my question. So I will go ahead and yield to the Ranking Member, Mr. Richmond, for the question he may have.

Mr. RICHMOND. Thank you, Mr. Chairman. I only have one, and it is for you, Ms. Grover.

Last year GAO recommended that TSA conduct comparison tests to determine whether passenger screening canines perform better in the passenger screening environment than traditional explosive detection canine teams. Have you all conducted that test? If so, what is the result? If not, when will you conduct it?

Ms. GROVER. Thank you, sir. We did recommend that TSA compare the effectiveness of the PSC canines to the conventional canines. They have not done so yet.

It is our hope that they will do so as soon as is reasonably possible because the PSC canines do cost more to deploy. They cost more to start up and then they cost more to maintain on an annual basis. So it is important to determine that they offer an enhanced benefit relative to the conventional canines, which are less expensive.

Mr. RICHMOND. Would anyone like to say if and when we are going to do that?

Ms. HARVEY. Yes, sir. So we have received—we always appreciate GAO's advice on this. We—from a training philosophy standpoint we believe that we should train our resources to operate in the environment where we are going to deploy them.

For passenger screening canine they get an extra 2 weeks of training. They cost about $18,000 more than traditional canine in the initial year and then $4,000 more in the out-years based on its additional certification. They receive specific training in terms of how to operate in and around passengers. Again, it is a training philosophy problem that we have with GAO's recommendation.

That said, I have asked DHS S&T to give us an analysis of the feasibility of conducting such a study with two concerns. One, the traditional canine aren't—we don't necessarily look at the breed or suitability of that canine for working in and around people. So I have concerns about bites.

So we need to be very careful about the teams that we pick as well as the protocols that we choose. We—S&T is going to give us a feasibility study on that sometime in the next 30 days.

Mr. RICHMOND. Thank you. Thank you all for being here.

Mr. Chairman, I yield back.

Mr. HUDSON. Thank the gentleman. I will recognize Mr. Rogers for any additional questions.

Mr. ROGERS. Thank you, Mr. Chairman.

Ms. Harvey, what do you mean by traditional canine? I have heard you use the word conventional also.

Ms. HARVEY. Sir, the traditional or conventional. I mean the traditional explosive detection canine that are trained to screen inanimate objects and are not specifically trained to screen people.

Mr. ROGERS. Not the vapor wake?

Ms. HARVEY. Correct.

Mr. ROGERS. Great.

How many—you know you talked about you finished your pilot study and now you are looking toward rolling out this on a broader scale. Do you have a time line now that you think you will be able to grow this program substantially?

Ms. HARVEY. Sir, are you referring to passenger screening canine?

Mr. ROGERS. Passenger screening canines who probably will have to be mostly private, given the capacity of limitations you are going to have inside TSA.

Ms. HARVEY. So we have allocated all of the teams that we currently have funding for. That is 144 passenger screening canine team. We have the in-house capability to provide the canines and the training for that amount.

Mr. ROGERS. If money were not your concern, and it is not, it is our concern, how many do you need?

Ms. HARVEY. That is a good question, sir.

Mr. ROGERS. Airports. Let's don't even talk about trains and bus stations and——

Ms. HARVEY. Sure.

Mr. ROGERS [continuing]. Freight. Just for airplanes.

Ms. HARVEY. So currently we are at 19 out of 28 CAT X airports. So if we wanted to deploy these teams to all the CAT X airports we would need whatever that number is, 32 additional teams.

Mr. ROGERS. Then to go beyond Category X airports, I guess you would like to go there, too, wouldn't you? As the next natural progression in this process.

Ms. HARVEY. We will—our approach is we will—every additional team that we get, we will apply it to the highest-risk airport that is left that doesn't have that capability. So we will just march down that list as we receive additional teams.

Mr. ROGERS. I would ask, for the record, if you will go back and look and see how much more money you think you would need to cover the balance of the Category X airports. Give me an idea about—for the committee, the idea how much it would cost and how many teams. Or just how many teams——

Ms. HARVEY. Okay.

Mr. ROGERS [continuing]. Not just about the cost.

Ms. HARVEY. Yes, sir.

Mr. ROGERS. Mr. Connell, you talked about wanting to use it for freight. I think that they are a great way for us to achieve a higher degree of scrutiny for freight. Have you had much interaction with TSA about this—these standards? You mentioned a little while ago that some of the private contractors were frustrated by the varying degrees of certification or criteria for certification. Is that accurate?

Mr. CONNELL. Correct. I mean I am not an expert on dogs, per se. But in surveying multiple vendors on kind of how the tests were run in 2011—and again not being an expert, there was just a common-sense approach of you know if you are going to run the test have a TSA dog go through it first to benchmark it that it works. Then have the private dog go after.

Mr. ROGERS. But now, Ms. Lontz, didn't you say——

Mr. CONNELL. That is my impression that did not happen.

Mr. ROGERS [coninuing]. Didn't you say a little while ago you now have an office of certification that you—maybe it wasn't Ms. Lontz. Maybe it was you, Ms. Harvey.

Ms. HARVEY. Yes. TSA certifies each of its teams that we deploy, whether it is led by a TSA handler or a law enforcement handler, and conducts an annual recertification as well.

Mr. ROGERS. So the concerns that Mr. Connell was expressing about providers getting frustrated that they were moving targets as far as criteria, that is no longer an issue?

Ms. HARVEY. I am unaware of that being an issue.

Mr. ROGERS. Okay.

Mr. Connell, do you think that using canines would help you fulfill 100 percent screening mandate that is always being asked for in your industry?

Mr. CONNELL. Correct. I think we are currently doing the 100 percent. But I think it will allow us to No. 1, do it better; to do it more efficiently; and No. 3, do it where it can control costs in such a way that it can only help the consumer pricing to be better controlled.

Mr. ROGERS. So as far as your industry being able to reach out to third-party providers, the only thing—and I could be misinterpreting what you were saying. The only thing standing in the way is the certification process by TSA. Is that correct?

Mr. CONNELL. Agreed. I would phrase it slightly different than that in that it allows us to go and find out what the true costs are to each facility. Forwarders teaming up together to you know chip in on the service, so to speak. But I would say you know having that ability to do so would allow us to take that next very large step forward and checking the economics of it.

Mr. ROGERS. Well, I just know that I have had, you know, FedEx, UPS, DHL all have expressed interest in being able to use this technology to meet their 100 percent screening, along with other things—other information and things that they use.

So I guess my question then to Ms. Harvey would be: Do you think that we are very close to the point that these third-party providers could in a pretty easy way access that certification process through your office so that they could provide this screening for these private freight providers?

Ms. HARVEY. Sir, I wouldn't say that we are exceptionally close to that decision. There are a lot of things that would need to be worked out in terms of roles and responsibilities. Who provides the explosives?

If TSA provides the explosives, we also need to provide oversight of how those explosives are handled. We need to work out rules and responsibilities in terms of certification and recertification every year, as well as training expectations, who is doing the training. No funding has been identified for this effort.

Mr. ROGERS. Well, let me close by saying anything I can do to help you, you let me know. Thank you.

Thank you all for being here.

Mr. HUDSON. Thank the gentleman. I thank the witnesses for indulging us. I am sorry the vote schedule kept you here a lot longer than you intended. I appreciate you hanging with us, and thank you for your testimony today.

Thank the Members for the good questions. Members of the subcommittee may have some additional questions for the witnesses, and I would ask that you respond to these in writing.

Without objection, subcommittee stands adjourned.

[Whereupon, at 3:58 p.m., the subcommittee was adjourned.]

APPENDIX

QUESTIONS SUBMITTED BY CHAIRMAN RICHARD HUDSON FOR MELANIE HARVEY

Question 1a. At the hearing, you stated that there were only 2 offices in TSA that lead the National Explosives Detection Canine Team Program (NEDCTP)—the Office of Security Operations and the Office of Law Enforcement/Federal Air Marshal Service. However, according to information provided by TSA, there are two additional offices within TSA that are responsible for some aspect of the canine program, specifically, the Office of Security Capabilities and the Office of Security Policy and Industry Engagement.

Can you identify the responsibilities each of these four offices has related to the NEDCTP?

Question 1b. While I understand each office may have a unique role to play, it would seem that in order to ensure efficiency and consistency across the spectrum of canine deployments, the responsibilities for the NEDCTP could be consolidated further.

Question 1c. Has TSA done an analysis to determine whether there are any roles and responsibilities that could be consolidated further for the NEDCTP?

Answer. The Transportation Security Administration's (TSA) Office of Security Operations (OSO) has overall responsibility for leadership of the National Explosive Detection Canine Team Program (NEDCTP). OSO manages the full range of the program including developing requirements, acquisition, program and financial management, allocation and deployment, canine operations, policy, performance measures, and field assessments.

The Office of Law Enforcement/Federal Air Marshal Service, Canine Training and Evaluation Section (CTES) supports NEDCTP's mission by providing training and certification for all canine teams. This includes selecting and training canines, training handlers, and conducting initial and recurrent certification of teams by field training visits and assessments. CTES ensures highly trained and capable handlers and canines, both Federal (TSA-lead teams) and non-Federal law enforcement, are deployed to detect and deter the introduction of explosives into our Nation's transportation system.

Many offices within TSA support NEDCTP in their respective areas of expertise. For example, TSA's Office of Security Capabilities Test and Evaluation group is a Department of Homeland Security-designated Operational Test Agent that provides independent expertise and resources using program-neutral policies to test and evaluate technologies, processes, and procedures. OSC provides this support across TSA for security technologies and capabilities, including to OSO for NEDCTP. The Office of Security Policy and Industry Engagement leads TSA's policy development and industry engagement and in 2011 played a major role in the Third-Party Canine pilot, which assessed industry's capability to use canine teams to screen air cargo. However, NEDCTP provided the canine subject-matter expertise for the initiative and is TSA's lead organization for all canine matters.

Question 1d. I understand the Office of Security Policy and Industry Engagement is responsible for discussing the issue of third-party certification with the air cargo industry; would this office also be responsible for implementing any such certification process, or would it be implemented by another office within TSA?

Answer. All canine certification activities are conducted by TSA's Office of Law Enforcement/Federal Air Marshal Service.

QUESTIONS SUBMITTED BY VICE CHAIRMAN MICHAEL D. ROGERS FOR MELANIE HARVEY AND ANNMARIE LONTZ

Question 1. Is TSA aware that the following Federal agencies have been using Third-Party Canine assets to protect critical infrastructure, Federal employees, and military personnel?

- Department of Defense
- Federal Protective Service
- Department of State
- Department of Homeland Security
- United States Marshalls
- Department of Energy
- Department of Treasury
- Internal Revenue Service
- National Park Service
- Multiple Federal Intelligence Agencies

Answer. Yes, the Transportation Security Administration (TSA) is aware of other Federal agencies' use of Third-Party Canine assets in support of their unique missions. Canine units vary in mission and operational environment. TSA is an active participant on the National Security Council—Transborder Security Sub-Interagency Policy Committee (Sub-IPC) on Working Dogs. This Sub-IPC is one forum at which Federal agencies with canine programs share information on their unique programs and missions, as well as best practices.

Question 2a. Is TSA aware these same agencies have testing and certification standards for use of Third-Party Cannes?

Has TSA spoken to these other agencies regarding their use of Third-Party Canines?

Question 2b. Why does TSA need to implement their own testing standards for Third-Party Canine operators? Are no other Federal standards sufficient to protect critical infrastructure or personnel?

Answer. The Transportation Security Administration (TSA) is aware that some of the Federal agencies rely on external resources for testing and certification of some of their canine teams. The North American Police Work Dog Association, United States Police Canine Association, International Police Work Association, and Auburn University are a few which offer various services in support of canine testing and certification.

TSA has spoken with many of these agencies on various aspects of their programs, including the environments in which they are deployed and how they are tested, certified, and regulated in support of their unique missions. Additionally, TSA is an active participant on the National Security Council (NSC)—Transborder Security Sub-Interagency Policy Committee (Sub-IPC) on Working Dogs. This Sub-IPC is one forum at which Federal agencies with canine programs share information and best practices.

The mission of the National Explosive Detection Canine Team Program (NEDCTP) is to deter and prevent explosives from entering the transportation system, including mitigating the threat to aviation. The margin of error for detection of a threat that can bring down an aircraft is much smaller than other agencies' threats. TSA's standards for training, testing, and certification of canine teams ensure that TSA is making the most efficient use of resources to mitigate that threat.

There are no Federal standards, and the standards used by the agencies listed above vary significantly from one organization to another in support of their unique missions. TSA continues to work as part of the Sub-IPC on Working Dogs which seeks to establish guidelines for Federal, State, local, and private-sector explosives detection canine assets. The guidelines were promulgated by the Sub-IPC to all Federal stakeholders for comment in July, and it is our understanding that they will be published in draft form for comment to stakeholders once Federal comments are adjudicated. When implemented, they could be used as a baseline standard to enhance interoperability and capabilities among the varying agencies.

Question 3. What are TSA's testing and certification standards for Third-Party Canines?

Answer. The Transportation Security Administration (TSA) has not set standards for the testing and certification of Third-Party Canines. In the event that the pilot is successful and results in a viable program, TSA will need to determine resource requirements and methodology, establish TSA and stakeholder roles and responsibilities, and implement any variation from TSA's current test and evaluation standards for Third-Party Canines.

○

www.ingramcontent.com/pod-product-compliance
Lightning Source LLC
Chambersburg PA
CBHW080624290526
45790CB00007B/2909